Challenging Common Core Language Arts Lessons

ADVANCED CURRICULUM FROM THE
CENTER FOR GIFTED EDUCATION AT WILLIAM & MARY

Challenging Common Core Language Arts Lessons

Activities and Extensions for Gifted and Advanced Learners in
GRADE 5

MAGDALENA FITZSIMMONS

William & Mary
School of Education

CENTER FOR GIFTED EDUCATION

P.O. Box 8795
Williamsburg, VA 23187

Copyright ©2016 Center for Gifted Education, William & Mary

Edited by Katy McDowall

Cover design by Raquel Trevino and layout design by Allegra Denbo

ISBN-13: 978-1-61821-552-9

At the time of this book's publication, all facts and figures cited are the most current available; all telephone numbers, addresses, and website URLs are accurate and active; all publications, organizations, websites, and other resources exist as described in this book; and all have been verified. The author and Prufrock Press make no warranty or guarantee concerning the information and materials given out by organizations or content found at websites, and we are not responsible for any changes that occur after this book's publication. If you find an error or believe that a resource listed here is not as described, please contact Prufrock Press.

Prufrock Press Inc.
P.O. Box 8813
Waco, TX 76714-8813
Phone: (800) 998-2208
Fax: (800) 240-0333
http://www.prufrock.com

TABLE OF CONTENTS

INTRODUCTION   1

Unit I: Journey to Success From Failure

Lesson 1.1: Creating Questions to Solve Problems   11
Lesson 1.2: Taking Note of Note-Taking   15
Lesson 1.3: Finding the Right Words   23
Lesson 1.4: Sharing Ideas With Infographics   27
Unit I: Culminating Essay Prompt   33

Unit II: The Hero's Journey

Lesson 2.1: A Hero Is Born   37
Lesson 2.2: The Hero's Journey Revealed   43
Lesson 2.3: Stops Along the Way   49
Lesson 2.4: Hero's Journey: The Battle Between Good and Evil   55
Lesson 2.5: What Is the Author's Message?   59
Unit II: Culminating Essay Prompt   66

Unit III: Journey Into Conflict

Lesson 3.1: Setting the Scene: New York During
            the American Revolution   69
Lesson 3.2: Who's Who in the American Revolution?   77
Lesson 3.3: The Inner and Outer Conflicts Caused by War   81
Lesson 3.4: Conflicting Reports   89
Lesson 3.5: Reporting the Revolution   99
Unit III: Culminating Essay Prompt   106

Unit IV: Journey as a Symbol for Change

Lesson 4.1: Reasons for the Journey   109
Lesson 4.2: The Informational Text Highway   117
Lesson 4.3: Voices Against Oppression   127
Lesson 4.4: Journey Through the Civil Rights Movement   133
Unit IV: Culminating Essay Prompt   141

ANSWER KEY   143

REFERENCES   147

ABOUT THE AUTHOR   149

COMMON CORE STATE STANDARDS ALIGNMENT   151

INTRODUCTION

The Common Core State Standards (CCSS) for English Language Arts (ELA) are K–12 curriculum standards that describe the English language arts skills and concepts students need to develop for success in higher education and the 21st-century workplace.

The College and Career Readiness Anchor Standards are the basis of the ELA/literacy standards. They specify the core knowledge and skills needed, while grade-specific standards provide specificity. The ELA standards also establish guidelines for literacy in history/social studies, science, and technical subjects for grades 6–12.

With the adoption of the CCSS in nearly every state, gifted and advanced learners need opportunities to master grade-level standards and ELA skills and concepts with greater depth, rigor, and understanding. This book is one of a series of books developed in conjunction with the Center for Gifted Education at William & Mary intended to give gifted and advanced learners additional practice and activities to master and engage with the CCSS for ELA. Each book in the series is organized by the content standards in one grade.

The lessons in this book cover grade 5 ELA content. In grade 5, the standards are addressed in five domains:

- Reading Literature and Informational Text,
- Foundational Skills,
- Language,
- Speaking and Listening, and
- Writing.

PURPOSE

The lessons in this book were written with the assumption that a teacher has already introduced ELA content standards through primary curriculum sources. Reading, writing, and speaking activities enrich and extend current grade-level ELA content rather than accelerate students to above-grade-level content. Each lesson focuses on multiple content standards, due to the overlap of skills inherent in ELA activities, and provides additional support and enrichment for gifted and advanced learners.

BOOK AND LESSON STRUCTURE

This book is divided into four units, each of which contains multiple lessons. Each unit focuses on a theme. Each unit centers on the ideas related to the theme within literature and nonfiction texts. Within the units, students will read, analyze, evaluate, and interpret poetry, short stories, and novels containing the theme. Students will demonstrate their growing understanding of this theme through various projects, narrative writing, informational writing, persuasive writing, and presentations.

Each lesson within a unit follows a predictable structure:

- The CCSS that are covered within the lesson are listed by number.
- Materials, including all student activity pages that are needed, are also listed. It is assumed students will have access to commonplace items such as pencils and paper, so the materials noted are those items that teachers will need to obtain/acquire in advance.
- Most required readings (except picture books, novels, and read-alouds) are available in the Appendix B: Text Exemplars and Sample Performance Tasks of the CCSS ELA document. (See additional information about text selection below.) It is anticipated that using these materials will allow for easy access to appropriate readings. In many cases, the readings that are used may come from the grade-level band above that of the grade level specified for the book.
- The lesson plan includes an estimate for the time it might take to complete the lesson; however, this will vary by teacher and classroom.
- The lesson objectives highlight what students will learn or be able to do as a result of completing the activities.
- An overview of the lesson's content provides a quick guide to the activities in which the students will be participating.
- A description of prior knowledge needed as a prerequisite for understanding the activities in a lesson is given. The teacher should be sure the students already have a working understanding of this content before beginning the lesson. Because the intended use of the activities is for students who have already mastered the stated standards, the teacher may want to preassess prior to having students complete the activities.
- The instructional sequence provides a detailed description of what the teacher and students will do during the lesson.
- The extension activities listed provide follow-up learning opportunities for students that go beyond the lesson to provide both additional enrichment and extension. Activities may be completed by individuals or groups, and may be completed at school or at home.
- At the end of each unit, a culminating essay is presented to provide closure and to assess students' synthesis of unit ideas.

THE SELECTION OF TEXT EXEMPLARS

The text exemplars selected for the book meet the specific criteria for high-ability learners suggested by Baskin and Harris (1980). These criteria (Center for Gifted Education, 2011) include:

- The language used in texts for the gifted should be rich, varied, precise, complex, and exciting.
- Texts should be chosen with a consideration of their open-endedness and their capacity to inspire thoughtful engagement.
- Texts for the gifted should be complex so that they promote interpretive and evaluative behaviors by readers.
- Texts for the gifted should help them develop problem-solving skills and acquire methods of productive thinking.
- Texts should provide characters as role models.
- Text types should cover a full range of materials and genres. (p. 15)

TOOLS FOR ANALYZING TEXTS

For several of the activities in this book, it is recommended that the teacher have students complete the Literature Analysis Model (see Figure 1) as part of their first encounter with the text. When students read the text for the first time, they should annotate it or use text coding (Harvey & Goudvis, 2007) as a metacognitive strategy to aid in comprehension. Once this marking of the text has occurred, the student should use the Literature Analysis Model and engage in a discussion about it (or selected portions) before progressing to other lesson activities.

The Literature Analysis Model encourages students to consider seven aspects of a selection they are reading: key words, tone, mood, imagery, symbolism, key ideas, and the structure of writing (Center for Gifted Education, 2011; McKeague, 2009; National Governors Association Center for Best Practices & Council of Chief State School Officers, 2010). After reading a selection, this model helps students to organize their initial responses and provides them with a basis for discussing the piece in small or large groups. Whenever possible, students should be allowed to underline and make notes as they read the material. After marking the text, they can organize their notes into the model.

Suggested questions for completing and discussing the model are:

- **Key words:** What words are important for understanding the selection? Which words did the author use for emphasis?
- **Important ideas:** What is the main idea of the selection? What are other important ideas in the selection?
- **Tone:** What is the attitude or what are the feelings of the author toward the subject of the selection? What words does the author use to indicate tone?

HANDOUT

Literature Analysis Model

Chosen or assigned text: _____	
Key words	
Important ideas	
Tone	
Mood	
Imagery	
Symbolism	
Structure of writing	

Figure 1. Literature Analysis Model. *Note.* Adapted from *Exploring America in the 1950s* (p. 10) by M. Sandling & K. L. Chandler, 2014, Waco, TX: Prufrock Press. Copyright 2014 by Center for Gifted Education. Adapted with permission.

- **Mood:** What emotions do you feel when reading the selection? How do the setting, images, objects, and details contribute to the mood?
- **Imagery:** What are examples of the descriptive language that is used to create sensory impressions in the selection?
- **Symbolism:** What symbols are used to represent other things?
- **Structure of writing:** What are some important characteristics of the way this piece is written? How do the parts of this selection fit together and relate to each other? How do structural elements contribute to the meaning of the piece?

After students have completed their Literature Analysis Models individually, they should compare their answers in small groups. These small groups may compile a composite model that includes the ideas of all members. Following the small-group work, teachers have several options for using the models. For instance, they may ask each group to report to the class, they may ask groups to post their composite models, or they may develop a new Literature Analysis Model with the class based on the small-group work. It is important for teachers to hold a whole-group discussion as the final aspect of implementing this model as a teaching-learning device. Teachers are also encouraged to display the selection on a document camera or overhead projector as it is discussed and make appropriate annotations. The teacher should record ideas, underline words listed, and call attention to student responses visually. The teacher should conclude the discussion by asking open-ended follow-up questions. For more information about analyzing literature, see Center for Gifted Education (2011).

GROUPING OPTIONS

The lessons in this book can be used for whole-group, small-group, and individual instruction.

Whole-Group Instruction

Teachers can use this book in one academic year in conjunction with the primary curriculum in a gifted education or advanced ELA class. All students would complete each lesson after being introduced to particular content standards. Teachers can integrate the lessons into the primary curriculum taught to a whole group and address higher order thinking questions through the lesson activities.

Small-Group Instruction

Teachers can use this book to differentiate learning in any ELA class by creating flexible student groups and giving students who need enrichment an opportunity for deeper understanding and engagement with a concept. Students can complete activities and practice at a self-guided pace with a partner or small group and engage in peer discussion, with or without directed supervision or intervention from the teacher.

Individual Instruction

The activities and questions in each lesson are a good way to determine individual understanding of a certain language arts concept on a deeper level.

AUTHOR'S RATIONALE FOR THE TEXTS AND THEMES SELECTED

I may not have gone where I intended to go,
but I think I have ended up where I needed to be.
—Douglas Adams, author and satirist

The concept of journey, in both the literal sense, physically moving from one place to another, and metaphorical sense, experiencing individual or societal transformation, has always fascinated me personally and professionally as a teacher working with students of all ages. When asked to write language arts lessons for gifted students and their teachers, I was inspired to use this concept as a springboard for the examination of journey as it occurs in a variety of literary genres.

Perhaps one of the most compelling stories of the 20th century was that of Ernest Shackleton's voyage to Antarctica, as recounted by Jennifer Armstrong in *Shipwreck at the Bottom of the World: The Extraordinary True Story of Shackleton and the Endurance*. Well-suited for the gifted classroom, this text is rich in figurative language, fascinating facts about the Antarctic, and written in an engaging, authentic style.

The hero's journey literary archetype is deeply embedded in cultures throughout the world, and is a concept with the depth and breadth worthy of investigation by high-ability students. I thought it would be interesting to use Madeleine L'Engle's *A Wrinkle in Time* as a focal point for the analysis of this archetype because it features a young girl as the protagonist and doubles as a work of science fiction. Additionally, the text is abundant with secondary themes, such as the challenges of adolescence, dystopian society, and the battle between good and evil.

The tale of the American Revolution, as told through the eyes of Sophia Calderwood in the historical fiction novel *Sophia's War* by Avi, is filled with the intensity and drama surrounding the conflict between England and the 13 colonies. Together with the Henry Wadsworth Longfellow poem "Paul Revere's Ride," the texts provide gifted students many opportunities for historical research and investigation.

Journey as a metaphor for change is exemplified by the historical nonfiction work *Freedom Walkers* by Russell Freedman. It is the story of the Montgomery Bus Boycott as experienced by ordinary people made famous by their participation in the Civil Rights Movement of the time. Rich with photographs, maps, quotes, and the timeline of events that led up to the Civil Rights Act of 1964, it serves as a cornerstone text for students leading to an in-depth understanding of how the Civil Rights Movement began.

In keeping with the current emphasis on preparing our students to be college and career ready, I have placed an emphasis on learning tasks that are collaborative in nature, make use of Web 2.0 tools and the Internet as a resource for information and creative production, and require students to communicate their ideas using a broad spectrum of visual, oral, and written products. In certain cases I have also included alternative texts that may be used in place of the anchor text. These include *Ice Story: Shackleton's Lost Expedition* by Elizabeth Cody Kimmel in Unit I and The Tripods trilogy by John Christopher, *The True Confessions of Charlotte Doyle* by Avi, *The Hobbit* by J. R. R. Tolkien, and *The Lightning Thief* by Rick Riordan in Unit II. It is my hope that you and your students find the lessons engaging, thought provoking, and challenging.

UNIT I

Journey to Success From Failure

This unit centers on the theme of how success can result from failure. Within the unit, students will read, analyze, evaluate, and interpret texts about the expeditions of Ernest Shackleton and his contemporaries and explore how their triumphs and failures contributed to discovery, learning, and personal growth. Students will consider ways in which it may be possible to learn more from failure than success. Students will demonstrate their growing understanding of this theme through various projects, research, informational writing, persuasive writing, and presentations.

LESSON 1.1
Creating Questions to Solve Problems

Common Core State Standards

- RI.5.1
- RI.5.3
- SL.5.1

Materials

- Lesson 1.1 Literature Analysis Model
- Student copies of *Shipwreck at the Bottom of the World: The Extraordinary True Story of Shackleton and the Endurance* by Jennifer Armstrong
- Student copies of *Ice Story: Shackleton's Lost Expedition* by Elizabeth Cody Kimmel (optional)
- Chart paper and markers for students

Estimated Time

- 40–50 minutes

Objectives

In this lesson, students will:
- make and explain inferences drawn from a text,
- demonstrate the ability to quote from a text when explaining what a text says explicitly, and
- use inferences drawn from a text in order to create a framework of questions that will guide further research on a topic.

Content

Students will discuss the outcome of Shackleton's voyage to the Antarctic and whether it can be considered a failure or a success. They will be presented with a research topic and will work in groups to generate research questions.

Prior Knowledge

Students will need to have read *Shipwreck at the Bottom of the World: The Extraordinary True Story of Shackleton and the Endurance* by Jennifer Armstrong. They should have participated in discussions about the book's events and analyzed the text for content-specific language. Students also will need to have the ability to make inferences and explain them using evidence from the text.

INSTRUCTIONAL SEQUENCE

1. Have students analyze at least one chapter of *Shipwreck at the Bottom of the World: The Extraordinary True Story of Shackleton and the Endurance* by Jennifer Armstrong using the

Literature Analysis Model. For an initial analysis, work with students to complete Lesson 1.1 Literature Analysis Model. You may wish to leave some of the boxes blank that may not be particularly relevant for this type of text. (See pp. 3–4 for additional information about using the Literature Analysis Model.)

2. As a class, discuss whether Shackleton's expedition to the Antarctic failed or succeeded. Guiding questions may include:
   - Did he accomplish his goal to cross Antarctica from "sea to sea"?
   - Was the fact that he managed to bring back every member of his crew alive even though the ship was crushed considered a success?
   - What are some ways it could be considered successful?
   - What are some ways it could be considered a failure?

3. Ask: *How might it be possible to learn more from failure than success?* Tell students that they will be researching this topic. Direct students to talk with a partner and create a list of what they consider to have been successes and failures that occurred on Shackleton's expedition. After students have completed their lists, generate a T-chart and list student responses.

4. Choosing one failure and one success, model how to create a research question that can be used to gather information. For example, one failure that occurred on the journey was that the ship got stuck in pack ice. Sample research questions about this failure include:
   - What information could Shackleton have used to avoid getting stuck in the pack ice?
   - What other tools could have been brought on the expedition to help release the ship from the pack ice?

5. Divide the class into groups of 3–4 and give each group a piece of chart paper and markers. Ask groups to create additional questions that could be used to answer the essential question and Shackleton's decisions as the expedition leader.

6. Allow at least 15 minutes for students to complete this task. Move around the groups to check on student progress, assess their understanding, and answer questions as needed.

7. When students have completed this task, create an anchor chart. Ask students to share the questions that they generated with their group. As students share their responses, ask them to explain why their question is a good one, citing examples from the text to support their choice. Display the anchor chart somewhere in the classroom where all students can see it.

Extension Activities

Students may:
- choose an explorer (other than Shackleton) and complete independent research on the success or failure of that explorer's expedition(s) and the possible reasons for the outcome; or
- write a brief narrative, recounting a time they experienced failure in trying to achieve a personal goal and what they learned from the experience.

Teacher's Note. Using the first extension activity, consider beginning the remaining lessons in the unit with a "Moment in Time" during which students can briefly share what they discovered about the explorer they researched.

NAME:_____ DATE:_____

LESSON 1.1
Literature Analysis Model

Directions: Complete this Literature Analysis Model about a chapter from *Shipwreck at the Bottom of the World: The Extraordinary True Story of Shackleton and the Endurance* by Jennifer Armstrong.

	Shipwreck at the Bottom of the World: Chapter _____
Key Words	
Important Ideas	
Tone	
Mood	
Imagery	
Symbolism	
Structure of Writing	

Note. Adapted from *Exploring America in the 1950s* (p. 10) by M. Sandling & K. L. Chandler, 2014, Waco, TX: Prufrock Press. Copyright 2014 by Center for Gifted Education. Adapted with permission.

LESSON 1.2

Taking Note of Note-Taking

Common Core State Standards

- W.5.8

Materials

- Lesson 1.2 *Shipwreck at the Bottom of the World* Online Research Project
- Lesson 1.2 Online Research Project: Suggested Resources (optional)
- Lesson 1.2 Notes Organizer
- Student copies of *Shipwreck at the Bottom of the World: The Extraordinary True Story of Shackleton and the Endurance* by Jennifer Armstrong
- Student copies of *Ice Story: Shackleton's Lost Expedition* by Elizabeth Cody Kimmel (optional)
- Computer and Internet access

Estimated Time

- 45–50 minutes (with additional time set aside for research)

Objectives

In this lesson, students will:
- gather relevant information from print and digital resources, and
- summarize or paraphrase information to conduct a research project.

Content

Students will be presented with a scenario-guided research project related to *Shipwreck at the Bottom of the World* by Jennifer Armstrong that they will work on for the remainder of the unit. They will develop their own research questions using questions created during Lesson 1.1. Effective note-taking strategies will be modeled, using one or more web resources. Using a notes organizer, students will practice the modeled strategy.

Prior Knowledge

Students will need to have prior experience in researching information on the Internet. Students also will need experience in sifting out important details from a text that are useful in researching a topic.

INSTRUCTIONAL SEQUENCE

1. Distribute Lesson 1.2 *Shipwreck at the Bottom of the World* Online Research Project and (optional) Lesson 1.2 Online Research Project: Suggested Resources. Break students into groups of 3–4 and discuss the project with the class.

Teacher's Note. Lesson 1.2 Online Research Project: Suggested Resources includes a list of possible web resources for students to use as they complete their research project. The websites are suggestions identified by the author and, because URLs may be updated or changed, alternative websites may be used at your discretion.

2. Allow students time to complete the research questions section of Lesson 1.2 *Shipwreck at the Bottom of the World* Online Research Project. Students should use questions they generated during Lesson 1.1. Additional questions to consider may include:
   - How did the preparations that the explorers made for their trips to the Antarctic affect the outcome of their expedition?
   - How did the mode of travel each explorer chose have an effect on whether or not the journey was successful?
   - How did the choice of a travel route make a difference in the outcome of any of the expeditions?
   - What were some of the personal beliefs or character traits of the expedition leaders that affected the outcome of the expedition in some way?
   - How did circumstances beyond the control of the explorers affect their journey to the Antarctic?

3. Distribute Lesson 1.2 Notes Organizer. Model how to complete the organizer, beginning by writing a research question in the left-hand column: *What were some of the personal beliefs or character traits of the expedition leaders that affected the outcome of the expedition in some way?* Choose a section from the exemplar text that has information that will help answer the question and model how to paraphrase the information.

4. Have students write the same question on their own organizer. Ask students to begin reading Chapter 1 of *Shipwreck at the Bottom of the World* and work with their group or with a partner to paraphrase the text and take notes relevant for answering the research question.

5. Allow students time to write a summary of their notes, and then ask groups to share their summaries with the rest of the class. Assess student understanding and clarify if necessary.

6. Students may use copies of Lesson 1.2 Notes Organizer to gather information to about each of their research questions.

Extension Activities

Students may:
- visit the National Geographic Young Explorers website (http://www.nationalgeographic. com/explorers/grants-programs/young-explorers) to investigate the kinds of companies

that fund expeditions and the kind of knowledge that is gained from them. They can use the knowledge gained from this investigation to inform their recommendations to Shackleton as outlined in the project scenario.

LESSON 1.2

Shipwreck at the Bottom of the World Online Research Project

SCENARIO

How might it be possible to learn more from failure than from success?

You are a wealthy English business owner and have just completed reading the amazing story of Ernest Shackleton's trip to the South Pole on the ship *Endurance*. Although Shackleton and the crew did not reach their destination and suffered countless hardships along the way, Shackleton managed to get every member of his crew back alive. It is now a few years after the fateful voyage of the *Endurance*, and Shackleton is seeking new sponsorship for another trip to the Antarctic. You would like to donate money toward this journey, because clearly Shackleton is a great leader. However, you want to make sure that this trip is more successful than the last.

TASKS

1. Your group is a committee of business owners interested in sponsoring Ernest Shackleton's next Antarctic exploration. Together you will research the Antarctic journeys of Shackleton and two other famous explorers of Shackleton's time, Roald Amundsen and Robert Falcon Scott.

2. Using online resources and Lesson 1.2 Notes Organizer, you will gather information about problems the expeditions faced that caused setbacks or failure. You will also record the successes of the expeditions and the strategies that resulted in success. Use the research questions that you created for Shackleton's journey as a basis for your research on all three of the explorers.

3. You will then compare the preparations and decisions made on each journey and create a list of 6–10 suggestions for what your group has determined are the best ways for Shackleton to ensure complete success on his next trip to the South Pole. Along with your suggestions, you will include reasons for them based on what you have learned about what did or did not work on the expeditions of Amundsen, Scott, and Shackleton.

4. Finally, by the end of this unit, your group will create a presentation for Shackleton, informing him that your committee is willing to help finance his next expedition if he follows your recommendations.

PRESENTATION OPTIONS

1. Infographic Presentation
   a. Create a multimedia infographic using Glogster (https://www.glogster.com).
   b. Create an infographic using traditional visual art materials such as poster paper, colored markers, pencils, and whatever other materials are available.

2. Multimedia Presentation
   a. Create a presentation using Padlet (https://padlet.com), Prezi (https://prezi.com), or Voice Thread (http://voicethread.com).

RESEARCH QUESTIONS

1.

2.

3.

Journey to Success From Failure

4.

5.

6.

7.

8.

NAME:_____ DATE:_____

LESSON 1.2
Online Research Project: Suggested Resources

Directions: The following are suggested web resources to help you gather information about the Antarctic and the Antarctic expeditions of Ernest Shackleton and the *Endurance*, Roald Amundsen and the *Fram*, and Robert Falcon Scott and the *Terra Nova*.

- "Pictures of Antarctica and the Arctic" by Cool Antarctica (http://www.cool antarctica.com/gallery/Antarctica_gallery_home.php)
- "Antarctica Fact File" by Cool Antarctica (http://www.coolantarctica.com/Antarctica%20fact%20file/antarctica-fact-file-index.php)
- "Antarctic History: A Time Line of the Exploration of Antarctica" by Cool Antarctica (http://www.coolantarctica.com/Antarctica%20fact%20file/History/exploration-history.php)
- Chapter 2 of *The South Pole* by Roald Amundsen (http://www.coolantarctica.com/Antarctica%20fact%20file/History/The_South_Pole/south_pole_amundsen_chapter2.htm)
- "Robert Falcon Scott–The Journey to the Pole" by Cool Antarctica (http://www.coolantarctica.com/Antarctica%20fact%20file/History/Robert-Falcon-Scott2.php)
- "A Changing Climate" by Discovering Antarctica (http://discoveringantarctica.org.uk/oceans-atmosphere-landscape/a-changing-climate)
- "The Race to the Pole" by Discovering Antarctica (http://discoveringantarctica.org.uk/science-and-exploration/journey-south/the-race-to-the-pole)
- "Scott's First Expedition to the Pole" by Royal Museums Greenwich (http://www.rmg.co.uk/discover/explore/south-pole-exploration-robert-falcon-scott-1901%E2%80%9304)
- "Quest for the South Pole" by Kelly Tyler (http://www.pbs.org/wgbh/nova/ancient/quest-south-pole.html)
- "Exploration Through the Ages" by The Mariners' Museum (http://ageofex.marinersmuseum.org)
- "The Endurance" by Kodak (http://www.kodak.com/US/en/corp/features/endurance)
- "Amundsen and Scott at the South Pole" by Peter Saundry (http://www.eoearth.org/view/article/150038)

For more information on each explorer, conducting a search on the Library of Congress website (https://www.loc.gov) is a great place to start.

LESSON 1.2
Notes Organizer

Directions: Using online resources and this organizer, you will gather information about your research questions. You may use multiple copies of the organizer to take as many notes as you need in order to complete your research. Choose one or two research questions to place on the organizer at a time.

Name of Explorer: _____	Group Name: _____
Source: _____	
Research Question:	**Notes (Answers to the Research Question):**
Summary:	

Journey to Success From Failure

LESSON 1.3
Finding the Right Words

Common Core State Standards

- RI.6.4
- L.6.6

Materials

- Lesson 1.3 Word Sort Vocabulary Cards (cut apart and place in envelopes; one envelope per pair of students)
- Student copies of *Shipwreck at the Bottom of the World: The Extraordinary True Story of Shackleton and the Endurance* by Jennifer Armstrong
- Student copies of *Ice Story: Shackleton's Lost Expedition* by Elizabeth Cody Kimmel (optional)
- Dictionaries or access to online dictionary

Estimated Time

- 40–50 minutes (with additional time set aside for research)

Objectives

In this lesson, students will:
- demonstrate their understanding of general academic and domain-specific words and phrases by categorizing them into groups for use in writing informational text.

Content

Students will use an open concept word sort strategy to organize domain-specific words into categories that align with topics related to their online research project.

Prior Knowledge

Students should be familiar with words and terms in *Shipwreck at the Bottom of the World: The Extraordinary True Story of Shackleton and the Endurance* by Jennifer Armstrong and related to the Antarctic and Antarctic exploration in general.

INSTRUCTIONAL SEQUENCE

1. Divide students into pairs and give each pair an envelope containing the vocabulary words from Lesson 1.3 Word Sort Vocabulary Cards. Ask them to take out the words and read them. They should be familiar with most of the words, but if not, ask them to use a dictionary or online dictionary to look up words that they do not know.

2. Explain to students that they will work with their partners to sort the words into categories that are meaningful to them or make sense in relation to the topic of their research. For example, the words *blizzard, gale, whiteout,* and *meteorologist* are all weather-related terms. The words *floe, glacier, growler, calving,* and *iceberg* all refer to ice. Allow at least 7–10 minutes for this task. Move between pairs to monitor student discussion, clarify understanding of the vocabulary words, or assist with determining categories.

3. When students have completed the word sort, ask them to do a "gallery walk" around the room to observe how other pairs of students sorted their words. Encourage them to note any similarities or differences between the word sorts.

4. Have students return to their seats and facilitate a brief discussion about the various categories they created for their word sorts and the reasons why they chose those categories. Clarify any misunderstandings as necessary.

5. Create an anchor chart listing the various categories and words associated with them. Explain to students that when they create their presentations they should consider using these words as part of their written suggestions to Shackleton, because they are important to understanding the topic of Antarctic exploration and will add authenticity to their final project.

6. To assess student understanding of the vocabulary, ask them to choose five of the words listed on the anchor chart and use each word in a sentence that directly relates to their research. An example might be "The enormous ice floes made it difficult for a ship to navigate through the icy waters." Ask students to briefly share their sentences with the person sitting next to them.

Extension Activities

Students may:

- read short articles or texts about explorations in other environments (e.g., desert, ocean, forest) and create cards for a word sort that are similar to the one they just completed, with words that are specific to the environment or the journey; or

- create a glossary of words used in this lesson, as well as any others that are relevant to their research topic, which may be included as part of the group presentation or be made available to future classes.

LESSON 1.3
Word Sort Vocabulary Cards

glaciers	sledge	expedition	growler
latitude	supply depot	plateau	floe
blizzard	continent	geography	gear
crew	navigation	chronometer	sextant
shelter	frostbite	frigid	gale
polar	climate	cargo	scurvy
meteorologist	terrain	calving	iceberg
lead	longitude	penguin	whiteout

Journey to Success From Failure

LESSON 1.4
Sharing Ideas With Infographics

Common Core State Standards

- W.6.4
- W.6.5
- W.6.6

Materials

- Lesson 1.4 Investigating Infographics
- Lesson 1.4 Rubric: Online Research Project Presentation
- Student copies of *Shipwreck at the Bottom of the World: The Extraordinary True Story of Shackleton and the Endurance* by Jennifer Armstrong
- Student copies of *Ice Story: Shackleton's Lost Expedition* by Elizabeth Cody Kimmel (optional)
- Computer and Internet access
- 4–5 examples of infographics (at stations)
- 4–5 markers, each a different color (at stations)
- 4–5 pieces of chart paper (at stations)
- Teacher's resources:
  - "Infographics" at Kids Discover (http://www.kidsdiscover.com/infographics)
  - "Infographics as a Creative Assessment" by Kathy Schrock (http://www.schrockguide.net/infographics-as-an-assessment.html)
  - "Tips for Making a Great Infographic" by LaToya Bailey (http://teacherweb.com/LA/helencoxhs/lmb/Tips-for-Making-a-Great-Infographic.pdf)

Estimated Time

- 50–60 minutes (with additional time set aside for research)

Objectives

In this lesson, students will:
- analyze the components of an infographic, and
- develop a presentation that has clear and coherent writing, content, organization, and style appropriate to task, purpose, and audience.

Content

Students will analyze examples of infographics to identify the characteristics they have individually and those they share in common. They will list their observations on anchor charts and then sort them into categories that have been identified as those elements that most well-developed infographics share. Students also will complete their online research project presentations.

Prior Knowledge

Students should have some knowledge of visual art elements, such as the definitions for color, space, balance, and contrast. Consult with the school's visual art teacher to make sure these topics have been covered in art class. Students also will need to be able to identify text features that enhance the reader's understanding of the text, such as illustrations, photographs, charts, graphs, or captions.

INSTRUCTIONAL SEQUENCE

1. Divide students into groups at stations with sample infographics. Tell students that they have 2–3 minutes to examine the infographic and list on the chart paper all of its characteristics, using the colored marker they were given.

2. When time is up, have each group rotate to the next station and continue to add their observations to the chart paper at their new station. Continue until students have had an opportunity to visit each station.

3. Display each station's chart paper so that it is visible to all students. Tell them that one way that people, companies, or organizations share information with the public is by creating infographics.

4. On a separate piece of chart paper or on the board, work with the class to list characteristics that each infographic has in common. Some of these may include use of color, font style, charts, maps, graphic organizers, data, informational text, photographs, or illustrations.

5. Distribute Lesson 1.4 Investigating Infographics. Tell students that most infographics share certain characteristics that make them effective at communicating information. Allow students to work in groups to organize what they recorded on chart paper at their stations into the categories listed on the handout.

6. When students have completed this task, facilitate a brief discussion about which of the infographics most effectively communicated information to the reader.

7. Tell students that many of the things they have learned in this lesson about effectively communicating information through text, graphics, and illustrations may be applied to creating presentations in other formats such as PowerPoint, Prezi, Glogster, and any others that are available.

8. At this point in the unit, students have all of the skills necessary to complete their group presentations. Groups should finish gathering information and use 2–3 days to create their presentations. Distribute Lesson 1.4 Rubric: Online Research Project Presentations as they work. Remind students that because several business groups will present their recommendations to Shackleton, it is important that each group creates a presentation with information that is clear and convincing.

Teacher's Note. An Exceeds Expectations column has been added to the rubric to encourage students to push themselves beyond the standard expectations. Very few students may rank in this column.

Extension Activities

Students may:

- visit the National Gallery of Art Kids Zone website (http://www.nga.gov/content/ngaweb/education/kids.html) to explore the interactives that encourage experimentation and creativity in the use of color, space, and pattern choice, which may serve as an excellent idea generator for an infographic design; or
- share the presentations they create by inviting other classes in for a gallery opening where groups will be available to answer questions about their presentation and how they researched the information for it and decided on its design elements.

LESSON 1.4
Investigating Infographics

Directions: There are five key components to an effective infographic. When viewing or creating an infographic, you should ask yourself:

1. What is the focus?

2. What information or facts are being presented?

3. What are the elements that support the reader's understanding?

4. Is there a part of the infographic that grabs the reader's attention?

5. Do the colors, text, and graphics enhance and support the information in the infographic?

Use this organizer to list the characteristics of the infographic that you determined were most successful in communicating information to the reader in each of the following categories.

Title: _____	
Topic	
Facts	

Title: _____

Elements That Support Understanding	
Attention Grabbers	
Colors and Graphics	

LESSON 1.4 RUBRIC
Online Research Project Presentation

	Exceeds Expectations 5 points	Proficient 4 points	Developed 3 points	Emerging 2 points	Novice 1 point
Research and Data	Thoroughly researched and supported by cited sources; includes additional information that enhances the topic.	Thoroughly researched and supported by cited sources.	Researched but not fully supported by cited sources.	Some information and data are included but are not supported by cited sources.	Minimal information and data are included, and the relationship to the topic is unclear.
Color Scheme	Carefully chosen colors support the content and message; greatly enhance the overall design.	Colors support the content and message.	Colors somewhat support the content and message.	Colors have minimal relationship to the content and message.	Colors seem randomly chosen and do not support the content.
Layout	Groups relevant data together and makes it easy for the reader to move from one piece of information to another; greatly enhances overall design.	Groups relevant data together and makes it easy for the reader to move from one piece of information to another.	Groups relevant data together so that the reader can follow the information shared.	Groups data together but it is somewhat confusing for the reader to follow.	Is confusing, making it difficult for a reader to follow information and determine the message.
Graphics	Reflect the theme of the presentation, making information very easy for the reader to follow and contribute significantly to the knowledge that is shared.	Reflect the theme of the presentation and inform the reader at a glance the knowledge about to be shared.	Mostly reflect the theme of the presentation and inform the reader about some of the information about to be shared.	Somewhat related to the theme of the presentation and do not always inform the reader about the information to be shared.	Have little to do with the theme of the presentation, making it difficult for the reader to determine the knowledge about to be shared.
Text	Chosen font greatly enhances the overall design and contributes significantly to the tone of the presentation.	Chosen font enhances the overall design and matches the tone of the presentation.	Chosen font matches the overall design and tone of the presentation.	Chosen font does not always match the overall design and tone of the presentation.	Chosen font does little to enhance the overall design and does not match the tone of the presentation.
					_____ / 20

Journey to Success From Failure

UNIT I
Culminating Essay Prompt

Directions: In this unit, you learned about successes and failures. Describe what you have discovered about how successes and failures can contribute to learning and personal growth. Make sure that you include some examples from your personal experiences.

UNIT II

The Hero's Journey

This unit centers on the themes related to the hero's journey, as recounted through the choices, events, and personal transformation experienced by the protagonist Meg in the novel *A Wrinkle in Time* by Madeleine L'Engle. Within the unit, students will read, analyze, evaluate, and interpret the novel and other texts that examine the hero's journey archetype. They will explore what it means to be a hero, a hero's role in society, and how an author communicates his or her message and important themes through a story. Students will demonstrate their growing understanding of this theme through various projects, narrative writing, informational writing, persuasive writing, and poetry.

LESSON 2.1
A Hero Is Born

Common Core State Standards

- L.6.5
- L.6.5.C
- SL.6.1

Materials

- Lesson 2.1 Literature Analysis Model
- Lesson 2.1 Hero Concept Organizer
- Lesson 2.1 Journey Concept Organizer
- Student copies of *A Wrinkle in Time* by Madeleine L'Engle
- Student copies of The Tripods trilogy by John Christopher, *The True Confessions of Charlotte Doyle* by Avi, *The Hobbit* by J. R. R. Tolkien, or *The Lightning Thief* by Rick Riordan (optional)
- Dictionaries (one per student or group)

Estimated Time

- 60 minutes

Objectives

In this lesson, students will:
- determine the connotations of words in order to provide a description of how a central idea is conveyed in a text.

Content

Students will engage in a discussion about the words *hero* and *journey*, both in terms of their literal meaning and as words that represent a larger concept that can be related to books they have read or films they have seen.

Prior Knowledge

Students will need to have read the first three chapters of *A Wrinkle in Time* by Madeleine L'Engle. They should have experience analyzing vocabulary and its relationship to concepts found in literature. Students also will need experience making inferences and explaining them using textual evidence.

INSTRUCTIONAL SEQUENCE

1. Have students analyze at least one chapter from *A Wrinkle in Time* by Madeleine L'Engle using the Literature Analysis Model. For an initial analysis of a chapter, work with students to complete Lesson 2.1 Literature Analysis Model. You may wish to leave some of the boxes blank that may not be particularly relevant for this type of text. (See pp. 3–4 for additional information about using the Literature Analysis Model.)

2. Introduce students to the term *hero*. Display the term on chart paper or on the board. Ask students to talk with a partner about what the word means to them.

3. Distribute Lesson 2.1 Hero Concept Organizer, explaining that they will use the handout to explore their meaning and the actual meaning of *hero*. Model how to complete the organizer using a think-aloud strategy. For example, when listing some people that one may consider a *hero*, discuss some of the qualities they possess that cause you to place them in that category. Allow students 5–7 minutes to complete the handout.

4. Ask students to share some of their answers with the rest of the class. Record answers on chart paper or display a copy of the handout.

5. Introduce students to the term *journey*. Display the term on chart paper or on the board. Once again, ask them to talk with a partner about what the word means to them.

6. Distribute Lesson 2.1 Journey Concept Organizer, allowing students 5–7 minutes to complete the handout.

7. Ask students to share some of their answers. Display student responses for both words where they can be easily seen.

8. Facilitate a brief discussion, noting similarities and differences between students' responses. Point out that the *connotation* (idea or feeling that a word invokes in addition to its literal meaning) of the words *hero* and *journey* can be different depending upon each individual's values, background, and prior experiences. Dr. Martin Luther King Jr. is considered a hero by many for his efforts to win civil rights for African Americans in spite of the risks to himself and his family. A lifeguard at the local beach may be considered a hero for saving a person from drowning. A journey for one person may be a daylong hike through a park while another person's journey might be a trip across the country. Guiding questions may include:

   - Are heroes always famous people?
   - Are heroes always physically strong?
   - Are heroes always considered "perfect" people without flaws?
   - Is a journey always a trip to another destination?
   - What is a "personal" journey?

9. Display the phrase *hero's journey* for the class. Ask students to predict, based on the definitions and discussions they have had about the two words during this lesson, what a *hero's journey* will look like in the novel *A Wrinkle in Time* by giving examples of what has occurred in the story thus far. (Meg reveals to Calvin that her father is missing. At the end of Chapter 3, Meg, Calvin, and Charles are suddenly whisked away to an unknown destination.)

Extension Activities

Students may:

- write a brief narrative placing themselves in the role of being a hero to someone else, describing what heroic act or acts they would perform and why; or

- create an infographic that illustrates the different types of heroes found in literature and film. Examples may include superheroes (Batman, The Fantastic Four), the unlikely hero (Frodo in *The Lord of the Rings*, Matilda, in the book of the same name by Roald Dahl), the antihero (Robin Hood), and the classical hero (Sir Lancelot). Ask them to make connections between the traits that these heroes share, as well as those that set them apart and perhaps are a reflection of society at the time they were created.

LESSON 2.1
Literature Analysis Model

Directions: Complete this Literature Analysis Model about a chapter from *A Wrinkle in Time* by Madeleine L'Engle.

	A Wrinkle in Time: Chapter _____
Key Words	
Important Ideas	
Tone	
Mood	
Imagery	
Symbolism	
Structure of Writing	

Note. Adapted from *Exploring America in the 1950s* (p. 10) by M. Sandling & K. L. Chandler, 2014, Waco, TX: Prufrock Press. Copyright 2014 by Center for Gifted Education. Adapted with permission.

LESSON 2.1
Hero Concept Organizer

Directions: Complete each of the boxes based on the word *hero*.

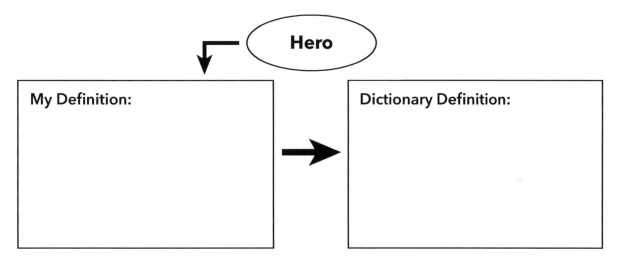

| Hero |
| My Definition: | Dictionary Definition: |

Heroes You Have Read About in Literature:

| Example: | People You Think Are Heroes: | Related Words/Phrases: |
| Nonexample: | | |

A Sentence Using the Word *Hero*:

LESSON 2.1
Journey Concept Organizer

Directions: Complete each of the boxes based on the word *journey*.

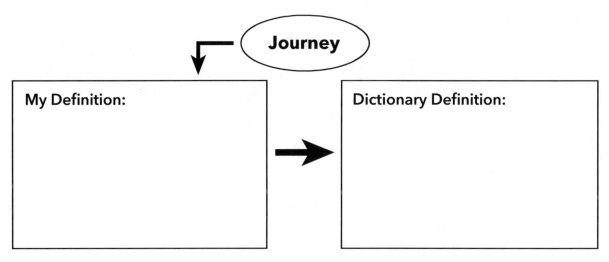

My Definition:

Dictionary Definition:

Journeys You Have Read About in Literature:

Example:

Nonexample:

Types of Journeys You Know About:

Related Words/Phrases:

A Sentence Using the Word *Journey*:

LESSON 2.2
The Hero's Journey Revealed

Common Core State Standards

- RL.6.1
- RL.6.5
- SL.6.1

Materials

- Lesson 2.2 Myths and the Hero's Journey
- Lesson 2.2. What Is a Hero's Journey?
- Student copies of *A Wrinkle in Time* by Madeleine L'Engle
- Student copies of The Tripods trilogy by John Christopher, *The True Confessions of Charlotte Doyle* by Avi, *The Hobbit* by J. R. R. Tolkien, or *The Lightning Thief* by Rick Riordan (optional)
- Student copies of "Theseus and the Minotaur" and "Jason and the Golden Fleece"

Estimated Time

- 90 minutes

Objectives

In this lesson, students will:
- determine elements of the hero's journey archetype by citing textual evidence to support analysis of inferences drawn from a text.

Content

Students will read the myths "Theseus and the Minotaur" and "Jason and the Golden Fleece," analyzing them for examples of the characteristics of heroes and journeys found within the texts.

Prior Knowledge

Students will need to have read Chapters 4–6 of *A Wrinkle in Time* by Madeleine L'Engle. Students should have experience making inferences and explaining them using textual evidence.

INSTRUCTIONAL SEQUENCE

1. Divide the class into groups of 3–4. Distribute copies of the myth "Theseus and the Minotaur" to half of the groups and "Jason and the Golden Fleece" to the other half. Allow students time to read the stories.

2. Afterward, distribute Lesson 2.2 Myths and the Hero's Journey. Ask students to work with their groups to answer the questions about the myth they just read. Allow 15–20 minutes for this task.

3. Have students share some of their responses and record them on a T-chart. Facilitate a brief discussion about whether they notice any commonalities between the two stories, particularly in terms of the character traits and actions of the hero, types of characters found in each story, and events and challenges the heroes encountered along their journeys.

   - For example, in both myths the protagonist, or "hero," encounters obstacles along the way toward a goal. Theseus sails away to the island of Crete in order to slay the Minotaur, who is responsible for the deaths of Athenians offered up for sacrifice to King Minos. Besides killing the Minotaur, he has to find his way out of a large maze in order to escape the island. Jason journeys to the land of Colchis, where he seeks the Golden Fleece, a task that is necessary in order for him to reclaim his throne. He too faces obstacles, such as having to yoke fire-breathing bulls, killing the dragon that protects the fleece, and overcoming an army of warriors that spring up from the dragon's teeth.

   - However, in each case, the heroes received assistance from someone. Ariadne helped Theseus by giving him the string so that he could find his way out of the maze, and Medea helped Jason escape Colchis with the fleece. Students should be able to identify character traits exhibited by both Theseus and Jason such as bravery, persistence, intelligence, and traits not necessarily associated with heroes such as deceit, despair and forgetfulness.

4. Explain to students that the myths they have just read are examples of a literary form, also referred to as an *archetype*, known as *hero's journey*, which represents a series of human experiences that form a pattern found in literature and film. Distribute Lesson 2.2 What Is a Hero's Journey?. Ask students to think of examples from literature, film, or television that might correlate with the different elements of the hero's journey archetype. Examples may include *Star Wars*, *The Wizard of Oz*, the Harry Potter series, or *The Lion King*.

5. Tell students that as they continue to read *A Wrinkle in Time*, they will be looking for the characteristics of this literary archetype. Ask: *Why do you think the concept of hero's journey emerged across time and cultures around the world and what message does it bring to society?* Answers might include the fact that human beings of all cultures value the basic character traits of a hero such as bravery, kindness, and perseverance through hardship, and yet in order to perform heroic acts, the hero must overcome obstacles and face danger or make a sacrifice.

Extension Activities

Students may:

- read about a historical figure who is generally considered a "hero" because of his or her actions or accomplishments and use a Venn diagram or T-chart graphic organizer to compare the hero archetype to the real-life hero; or

- visit "The Hero's Journey" by ReadWriteThink (http://www.readwritethink.org/files/resources/interactives/herosjourney) to complete a brief interactive task that explains the hero's journey.

> **Teacher's Note.** Historical figures to consider include Dr. Martin Luther King Jr., Harriet Tubman, Marie Curie, Nelson Mandela, Jonas Salk, Oskar Schindler, Susan B. Anthony, and many others.

LESSON 2.2
Myths and the Hero's Journey

Directions: After reading the myth "Theseus and the Minotaur" or "Jason and the Golden Fleece," complete the chart below using examples from the text to support your answers.

Myth Title: _____

Question	Textual Evidence
Who is the hero in this story? What are the hero's character traits?	
Does the hero go on a journey? What are some of the challenges the hero faces along the way?	
Does the hero have someone to help him? If so, describe who that person is and how he or she provides help.	
Does the hero face a major obstacle during his journey? Describe what it is and whether or not the hero was able to overcome it.	
Does the hero return home from the journey? Does anyone help him to do this, and if so, how do they provide assistance?	
Describe what you think the hero has learned from his experiences on the journey.	

The Hero's Journey

LESSON 2.2
What Is a Hero's Journey?

Directions: Use the chart below to help you identify the different elements of the hero's journey.

Hero's Journey Elements	What Happens in the Story
Departure	The hero may begin his or her journey a number of different ways, but it usually starts with an event that is traumatic or disturbing. Sometimes the hero will go on the journey willingly, and other times the hero may have to be tricked or convinced to go.
Initiation and the Road of Trials	The hero leaves what is safe and familiar and begins the journey. Along the way he will face trials or obstacles that he must overcome in order to succeed and achieve his goal. Along the way the hero might meet a person who will act as a mentor, giving him help along the way. Sometimes this character has magical powers.
Innermost Cave	The innermost cave might represent an actual place where the hero must face his or her greatest danger or obstacle, or it may represent an inner conflict that the hero experiences and must overcome in order to succeed in reaching his goal. This may be the point at which the hero faces a terrible enemy and possible death.
Return	The hero returns home, again sometimes willingly and other times unwillingly. The hero brings newfound wisdom with him and may strive to reconcile with those he left behind.

The Hero's Journey

LESSON 2.3
Stops Along the Way

Common Core State Standards

- RL.6.1
- RL.6.3
- RL.6.4
- RL.6.5
- W.6.4
- W.6.7

Materials

- Lesson 2.3 *A Wrinkle in Time* 2-5-8 Menu
- Lesson 2.3 Rubric: 2-5-8 Menu
- Student copies of *A Wrinkle in Time* by Madeleine L'Engle
- Student copies of The Tripods trilogy by John Christopher, *The True Confessions of Charlotte Doyle* by Avi, *The Hobbit* by J. R. R. Tolkien, or *The Lightning Thief* by Rick Riordan (optional)
- Computer and Internet access
- Materials as needed for creating a collage, such as scissors, glue, used magazines, and construction paper (optional)
- Materials to create a board game, such as board game templates, crayons, markers, colored pencils, construction paper, cardboard, scissors, and glue (optional)

> ***Teacher's Note.*** As much as possible, try to have the materials located in specific centers around the classroom so that they are easily available to students as needed while they engage in independent work.

Estimated Time

- 50–90 minutes (with additional time set aside for projects)

Objectives

In this lesson, students will:
- cite textual evidence in order to demonstrate understanding of what the text says explicitly as well as inferences drawn from the text;
- determine the meaning of words and phrases as they are used in a text, including figurative and connotative meanings;
- analyze the impact of a specific word choice on meaning and tone;

- describe how a particular story's or drama's plot unfolds in a series of episodes as well as how the characters respond or change as the plot moves toward a resolution; and/or
- compare and contrast two or more characters in a story, drawing on specific details in the text (e.g., how characters interact).

Content

Students will complete a 2-5-8 menu of learning tasks related to the content and themes of *A Wrinkle in Time* by Madeleine L'Engle. They may choose the tasks they wish to complete as they continue to read the novel.

Prior Knowledge

Students will need to have read Chapters 7–11 of *A Wrinkle in Time* by Madeleine L'Engle. Students will need experience making inferences and explaining them using textual evidence. They will need to be able to work independently to complete a series of short research tasks. Students should have prior knowledge of the term "glossary" and its purpose.

INSTRUCTIONAL SEQUENCE

1. Distribute Lesson 2.3 *A Wrinkle in Time* 2-5-8 Menu. Tell students that they will complete at least two tasks of their choice. The task point value must add up to 10 points and they are responsible for completing these tasks independently as part of their work for this unit.
2. Go over the menu with the class to determine if modeling of any of the tasks is required. For example, it may be necessary to show a few examples of board games in order for students to understand its various components, or what makes a board game fun and engaging. Students may not be familiar with the term *collage*, so a few examples of this type of visual art would be helpful for students to see.

Teacher's Note. Board game templates can be found online, such as at Donna Young.org (http://www.donna young.org/homeschooling/games/game-boards.htm). A collage interactive can be accessed on the National Gallery of Art Kids Zone website (https://www.nga.gov/kids/zone/collagemachine.htm).

3. Share with students that during small-group instruction (when the teacher is working with a small group and the rest of the class is tasked with other language arts activities to complete), they will have an opportunity to work on completing their menu tasks as part of their independent work time.
4. Distribute Lesson 2.3 Rubric: 2-5-8 Menu to students and review the expectations for completion of the tasks and answer any questions as necessary. Depending on how much time is set aside for completing this unit, assign students a due date for the menu tasks.

Extension Activities

Students may:

- choose to apply one or more of the menu tasks to another text;
- write an alternate ending to *A Wrinkle in Time* that takes the plot in a different direction (e.g., what would have happened if Meg was unable to save Charles?); or
- complete more than the required number of tasks on the menu.

LESSON 2.3
A Wrinkle in Time 2-5-8 Menu

Directions: Choose at least two tasks from the following menu. The combined value of the tasks must equal 10 points. Place a checkmark next to the ones you will complete. All tasks must be completed by _____.

2 Points

❏ Create a collage of words and pictures that relate to the concept of the hero's journey.

❏ Complete a character web that shows how Meg in *A Wrinkle in Time* demonstrates that she is a hero.

❏ Create a glossary of 20 words from *A Wrinkle in Time* that you think are important for a reader to understand while reading the book.

5 Points

❏ Write a diamante poem with the name of one of the characters from *A Wrinkle in Time* in the first line and the name of another character in the last line. Use what you have learned about the characters from reading the book to complete your poem.

❏ In order to help readers visualize a scene or setting in a story, authors often use figurative language and sensory details. These might include similes, metaphors, personification, and words that describe what a character hears, sees, feels, or touches. Madeleine L'Engle uses a variety of these techniques in *A Wrinkle in Time*. Create a poster, chart, or infographic that lists at least eight different examples of figurative or sensory language found in *A Wrinkle in Time* and give examples from the text for each.

❏ Choose three of your favorite chapters from *A Wrinkle in Time*, one from the beginning of the book, one from the middle, and one from the end. Retell what happens in each chapter from the first-person point of view of one of the characters, writing as if the character was making an entry into a diary or journal. Include an illustration of an important scene from each chapter as part of the journal entry.

8 Points

❑ Design a board game called *A Wrinkle in Time* Hero's Journey. Your game should include all of the events in the book that correspond with the elements of the hero's journey archetype, as well as the various characters encountered in the story. Be sure to include rules written in complete sentences, game pieces, and dice or a spinner for your game.

❑ *A Wrinkle in Time* is a work of science fiction. Research to discover the elements of the science fiction genre and write a book review that explains why this book is a good example of that genre. Be sure to include the following elements in your review:
  • Begin your review with an opening statement about the book that includes its title, author, genre (science fiction), and the age range of the reader.
  • Give a general summary of the book without giving away too many details.
  • Talk about why you think this book is a good example of the science fiction genre, using some details from the text to support your opinion.
  • Conclude, summarizing why you think the book is a good example of science fiction and why it should be included in every school's library.

LESSON 2.3 RUBRIC
2-5-8 Menu

	Exceeds Expectations 5 points	Proficient 4 points	Developed 3 points	Emerging 2 points	Novice 1 point
Knowledge and Understanding	Reflects a deep understanding and mastery of unit concepts and skills.	Reflects a good understanding and mastery of unit concepts and skills.	Reflects an understanding of unit concepts and skills.	Reflects some understanding of unit concepts and skills.	Reflects little understanding of unit concepts and skills.
Craftsmanship and Completion	Requirements for all of the chosen tasks have been completed; work is of the highest quality and shows care and thoughtfulness beyond expectations.	Requirements for all of the chosen tasks have been completed; work is high quality and shows care and thoughtfulness.	Requirements for most of the chosen tasks have been completed; work is mostly good quality and shows some care and thoughtfulness.	Requirements for some of the chosen tasks have been completed; work shows quality, care, and thoughtfulness.	Requirements for few of the chosen tasks have been completed; much of the work does not show quality, care, and thoughtfulness.
					_____ / 8

LESSON 2.4

Hero's Journey: The Battle Between Good and Evil

Common Core State Standards

- RL.6.1
- SL.6.1.A–D

Materials

- Lesson 2.4 Socratic Seminar: Participation Evaluation
- Student copies of *A Wrinkle in Time* by Madeleine L'Engle
- Student copies of The Tripods trilogy by John Christopher, *The True Confessions of Charlotte Doyle* by Avi, *The Hobbit* by J. R. R. Tolkien, or *The Lightning Thief* by Rick Riordan (optional)
- Computer and Internet access
- Teacher's resources:
  - "Socratic Seminars" by ReadWriteThink (http://www.readwritethink.org/professional-development/strategy-guides/socratic-seminars-30600.html)
  - "Socratic Seminars: Patience & Practice" by Teaching Channel (https://www.teachingchannel.org/videos/bring-socratic-seminars-to-the-classroom)

Estimated Time

- 90–100 minutes

Objectives

In this lesson, students will:
- cite textual evidence in order to demonstrate understanding of what the text says explicitly as well as inferences drawn from the text.

Content

Themes encountered in the hero's journey archetype and the science fiction and fantasy genres often include a conflict between good and evil. Students will participate in a Socratic Seminar to discuss how the theme of good versus evil presents itself in *A Wrinkle in Time* and its role as part of the hero's journey archetype.

Prior Knowledge

Students should have read up to Chapter 11 of *A Wrinkle in Time* by Madeleine L'Engle. Students will need experience making inferences and explaining them using textual evidence. They will need some experience with the Socratic Seminar as a discussion format.

INSTRUCTIONAL SEQUENCE

1. Ask students: *When I say the phrase "the battle between good and evil," what is the first thing that comes to mind?* Have students talk with a partner for a few minutes and discuss their answers. Facilitate a brief class discussion about what this phrase means, both in terms of literature and films, as well as real-life examples. Consider recording student responses and displaying them.

2. Ask students whether they have encountered examples of good versus evil in *A Wrinkle in Time* (the first references to evil occur in Chapter 4 of the book). Tell students that they will participate in a Socratic Seminar to discuss how the conflict between good and evil emerges in the story and what impact it has on the sequence of events and the hero's journey archetype.

3. Ask students to reread Chapters 4–9, noting aspects of the story that refer to concepts of good and evil. They should write down the examples with page numbers in a reading journal or graphic organizer. Students may work in groups or with a partner. Allow at least 30–40 minutes for this task. Sample responses may include:

   - **Chapter 4:** *"What could there be about a shadow that was so terrible that she knew that there had never been before or ever would be again, anything that would chill her with a fear that was beyond shuddering, beyond crying or screaming, beyond the possibility of comfort?"* Meg is looking at the dark shadow that her father is fighting and is terrified by it. By using words like "fear," "shuddering," "screaming," and "crying," the author creates a sense for the reader that the shadow is something to be feared, or "evil."

   - **Chapter 5:** *"But what is it?" Calvin demanded. "We know that it's evil, but what is it?" "Yyouu hhave ssaid itt!" Mrs. Which's voice rang out. "Itt iss Eevill. Itt iss thee Ppowers of Ddarrkknesss!"* This is where Meg, Charles, and Calvin see that the dark shadow also surrounds the Earth. This makes them realize that everything that is important to them may be at risk and in danger.

   - **Chapter 6:** *"Suddenly there was a great burst of light through the Darkness. The light spread out and where it touched the Darkness the Darkness disappeared. The light spread until the patch of the Dark Thing had vanished, and there was only a gentle shining, and through the shining came the stars, clear and pure."* The Medium shows Meg, Charles, and Calvin that the Darkness, or "evil" can be overcome by "light," the light representing "good."

4. When conducting the Socratic Seminar, discussion groups should consist of no more than eight students at once. If the class is large, split students into 2–3 groups, with the students who are not participating in the discussion sitting in a circle on the outside of the group. In order for every student to have an opportunity to speak, teachers should limit the discussion to 15–20 minutes per group.

5. Students sitting in the outside circle may serve as peer evaluators for the quality of discussion that takes place. Distribute Lesson 2.4 Socratic Seminar: Participation Evaluation for students to record the participation of a partner in the inner circle of the Socratic Seminar. When the inner circle of students has had their opportunity to speak, have them switch places with the outer circle and repeat the process.

> **Teacher's Note.** If there is more than one discussion group, assign each group a selection of the assigned chapters to focus on so that each group's discussion content varies.

6. Lead the seminar, asking students open-ended questions that relate to the theme of good versus evil in the story. Be sure to create these questions ahead of time, ensuring that they will result in a variety of student responses. Questions may include:

   ▪ In Chapter 4 of *A Wrinkle in Time*, how does the author let the reader know that Meg, Charles, and Calvin are about to encounter "evil" in their journey to find Meg's father?

   ▪ Mrs. Whatsit mentions in Chapter 5 that some of the greatest fighters of the "powers of darkness" have been people like Leonardo Da Vinci, Mahatma Gandhi, Albert Einstein, and others. What characteristics do these people have that make them a "fighter" of darkness?

   ▪ In Chapter 6, the Medium uses the crystal ball to show Calvin an image of his mother in order to reassure him that she is all right. What does he see, and why do you think Meg "took his hand in hers" after seeing what they witnessed?

   ▪ In Chapter 6, when Meg, Charles, and Calvin land on Camazotz, they encounter a little boy awkwardly bouncing a ball in front of his house. When the boy's mother notices he is outside she hurriedly rushes him inside, causing the boy to drop the ball. When Charles tries to return the ball to the mother she refuses it, denying that it belongs to her son. Based on what the children have already observed about the inhabitants of the planet, how would you explain the mother's actions?

Extension Activities

Students may:

▪ read the Scholastic interview with author Madeleine L'Engle (http://www.scholastic.com/teachers/article/madeleine-l39engle-interview-transcript) and share their findings with the class, focusing on how the author got her idea for *A Wrinkle in Time*, her ideas about good and evil, and why they should be shared with children; or

▪ create a storyboard with illustrations that represent a scene from another novel or movie they have seen that represents a confrontation between good and evil.

NAME:_____ DATE:_____

LESSON 2.4
Socratic Seminar: Participation Evaluation

Directions: During the seminar, listen attentively and respond to one another with respect. Before agreeing or disagreeing with a classmate, summarize that classmate's ideas/opinions, and then express your own clearly and with supporting evidence from the text. Place a check in the appropriate spaces based on the level of participation you observed from your partner.

Partner's Name: _____

1. Number of comments they shared:
   a. No comments _____
   b. 1 comment _____
   c. 2 comments _____
   d. 3 comments _____
   e. 4 or more comments _____

2. Quality of speaking points:
   a. No comments _____
   b. Just repeats others' ideas _____
   c. Expresses original ideas _____
   d. Original, deep comments, new ideas _____

3. References to text:
   a. No references _____
   b. 1–2 references _____
   c. 3 references _____
   d. 4 or more references _____

Positive suggestions or comments:

The Hero's Journey

NAME:_____ DATE:_____

The Hero's Journey

LESSON 2.4
Socratic Seminar: Participation Evaluation

Directions: During the seminar, listen attentively and respond to one another with respect. Before agreeing or disagreeing with a classmate, summarize that classmate's ideas/opinions, and then express your own clearly and with supporting evidence from the text. Place a check in the appropriate spaces based on the level of participation you observed from your partner.

Partner's Name: _____

1. Number of comments they shared:
   a. No comments _____
   b. 1 comment _____
   c. 2 comments _____
   d. 3 comments _____
   e. 4 or more comments _____

2. Quality of speaking points:
   a. No comments _____
   b. Just repeats others' ideas _____
   c. Expresses original ideas _____
   d. Original, deep comments, new ideas _____

3. References to text:
   a. No references _____
   b. 1–2 references _____
   c. 3 references _____
   d. 4 or more references _____

Positive suggestions or comments:

Challenging Common Core Language Arts Lessons: Grade 5 © Prufrock Press Inc.
Permission is granted to photocopy or reproduce this page for single classroom use only.

LESSON 2.5
What Is the Author's Message?

Common Core State Standards

- RL.6.1
- W.6.2
- W.6.4

Materials

- Lesson 2.5 Hero's Journey Organizer (optional)
- Lesson 2.5 Literary Essay Organizer
- Lesson 2.5 Peer Feedback
- Lesson 2.5 Rubric: Literary Essay
- Student copies of *A Wrinkle in Time* by Madeleine L'Engle
- Student copies of The Tripods trilogy by John Christopher, *The True Confessions of Charlotte Doyle* by Avi, *The Hobbit* by J. R. R. Tolkien, or *The Lightning Thief* by Rick Riordan (optional)
- Computer and Internet access

Estimated Time

- 90 minutes (with additional time set aside for writing)

Objectives

In this lesson, students will:
- demonstrate understanding of a theme or central idea of a text and how it is conveyed through particular details by writing to communicate ideas and concepts.

Content

Students will generate a literary essay, examining Meg's transformation in *A Wrinkle in Time*.

Prior Knowledge

Students will need to have completed reading *A Wrinkle in Time* by Madeleine L'Engle. They will need experience making inferences and explaining them using textual evidence. Students should be familiar with the format of a literary essay.

INSTRUCTIONAL SEQUENCE

1. Explain to students that authors are able to convey messages about their personal beliefs through the stories they tell. Facilitate a brief discussion about this idea using a previously

read text that students are familiar with, such as *Henry's Freedom Box* by Ellen Levin (freedom, justice, perseverance), *Freedom Summer* by Deborah Wiles (freedom, prejudice), *Each Little Bird That Sings* by Deborah Wiles (loyalty, remaining true to personal beliefs), or *Ruby's Wish* by Shirin Yim Bridges (determination, equality for girls). Guiding questions may include:

- What is the author's message in this book?
- How does the author convey his or her message through the actions of the characters?
- At which point in the story were you aware that the author was trying to send a message to the reader?

2. Re-examine the structure of the hero's journey by visiting "The Hero's Journey" interactive at ReadWriteThink (http://www.readwritethink.org/classroom-resources/lesson-plans/preparing-journey-introduction-hero-1152.html). Ask students to work with a partner to complete the interactive by identifying Meg as the heroine and events from *A Wrinkle in Time* to describe each stage of the Hero's Journey. Students may complete Lesson 2.5 Hero's Journey Organizer as they go through the interactive or print their responses from the website.

Teacher's Note. If student computer access is not available, use a computer and projector to move through the interactive with students and have them complete the stages of Meg's journey using the Hero's Journey Organizer.

3. As a class, referring to the completed organizer, discuss how an author's message about personal transformation can be revealed through the hero's journey archetype, examining how Madeleine L'Engle shows Meg's transformation throughout the novel. Guiding questions may include:
   - What does "personal transformation" mean, and how does it relate to the character of Meg? (Personal transformation means changes a person goes through whether it is physical or changing their behaviors or the way they view the world around them. In this case, Meg undergoes changes in the way she feels about herself and what she is capable of as a person.)
   - How has the journey Meg has taken changed her from the person she was at the beginning of the story to the person that returned home with her father? (Meg starts out as being very insecure about herself and ends up bravely confronting IT at the end, thereby saving her brother Charles.)
   - How did each part of the Hero's Journey contribute to Meg's transformation? (As Meg faced and overcame each obstacle in the story, she became a stronger and braver person. For example, at the end of the story Meg realizes that she is the only person who can get Charles away from IT, since she has the closest relationship with him. However, she does not want to confront IT because she is afraid of failing. She finally overcomes her fears and saves her brother using her love to break the influence of IT.)

4. Share with students that they will write an essay that explains how Meg's experiences on the hero's journey changed her as a person, and how each stage of the journey revealed

the author's views about concepts such as human relationships, perseverance in the face of challenge, and individual rights.

5. Distribute Lesson 2.5 Literary Essay Organizer and Lesson 2.5 Rubric: Literary Essay. Tell students that they will use the organizer to help them write the first draft of their essays. They can also refer to the rubric as needed.

6. After students complete their first draft, distribute Lesson 2.5 Peer Feedback for students to evaluate each other's essays in order to improve their writing.

Extension Activities

Students may:

- use the graphic organizer they used to write their essay as the basis for creating an infographic that illustrates the stages of Meg's hero's journey.

LESSON 2.5
Hero's Journey Organizer

Directions: Identifying Meg as the heroine of *A Wrinkle in Time*, complete the following graphic organizer to show each stage of the hero's journey as Meg experienced it in the story.

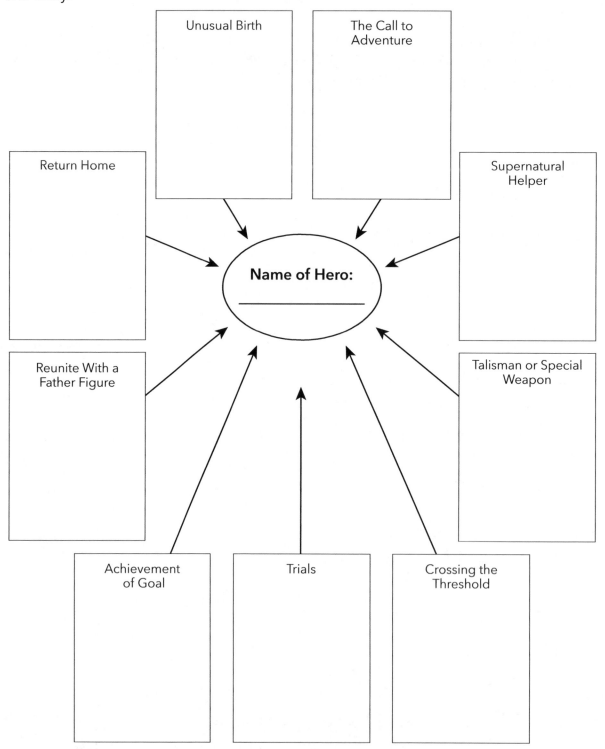

Challenging Common Core Language Arts Lessons: Grade 5 © Prufrock Press Inc.

The Hero's Journey

LESSON 2.5
Literary Essay Organizer

Directions: Use the organizer below to write an essay draft responding to the following question: *How did Meg's experiences on the "hero's journey" to rescue her father change her? What do you think she learned from those experiences?*

Introduction/ Opening Statement	
Paragraph 1: Supporting Details	
Paragraph 2: Supporting Details	
Paragraph 3: Supporting Details	
Conclusion	

The Hero's Journey

LESSON 2.5
Peer Feedback

Directions: Read the first draft of your partner's essay. Next, complete each section of this form, making sure your comments are positive and helpful. When you and your partner have both finished the form, have a conversation and share what you wrote about each other's essay.

The Hero's Journey

Peer's Name: _____	
Praise *What do you think is good about the essay? Did the writer have a strong opening? Was there support with details from the text? Be specific.*	
Question *Is there anything in the essay that is confusing? Do you have a question about a word or phrase the writer used?*	
Polish *What can your partner do to make his or her writing better?*	

LESSON 2.5 RUBRIC
Literary Essay

	Exceeds Expectations 5 points	Proficient 4 points	Developed 3 points	Emerging 2 points	Novice 1 point
Organization	Introduction clearly states the main topic; supporting information is relevant, strongly connected to the topic, presented in a logical order, and has a strong conclusion.	Introduction clearly states the main topic; supporting information is relevant, connected to the topic, and presented in a clear, logical order; there is a conclusion.	Introduction states the main topic; supporting information is mostly relevant, mostly connected to the topic, and information is presented in order; there is a conclusion.	Introduction states the main topic but is somewhat unclear; supporting information is moderately connected to the topic but not always presented in order; there is a weak conclusion.	Introduction is unclear; supporting information is not entirely relevant, connected to the topic, and not always presented in order; there is no conclusion.
Details	Clear, well researched, and greatly enhance the reader's understanding of the topic.	Clear, well researched, and enhance the reader's understanding of the topic.	Clear and support the reader's understanding of the topic.	Not always clear and not always supportive of the reader's understanding of the topic.	Not clear and do little to support the reader's understanding of the topic.
Word Choice	Outstanding use of vivid words and phrases; word choice is accurate, clear, and reflects extensive knowledge of the topic.	Excellent use of vivid words and phrases; word choice is accurate, clear, and reflects solid knowledge of the topic.	Good use of vivid words and phrases; word choice is mostly accurate, clear, and reflects knowledge of the topic.	Fair use of vivid words and phrases; word choice is sometimes accurate and reflects partial knowledge of the topic.	Little use of vivid words and phrases; word choice is mostly inaccurate, and reflects lack of knowledge about the topic.
Sentence Structure, Grammar, Mechanics, and Spelling	Sentence structure is outstanding, greatly contributing to the effectiveness of the writing with no errors in grammar, mechanics, and spelling.	Sentence structure is excellent, contributing to the effectiveness of the writing with almost no errors in grammar, mechanics, and spelling.	Sentence structure is good, contributing to the effectiveness of the writing with some errors in grammar, mechanics, and spelling.	Sentence structure is fair, making the writing somewhat confusing for the reader; numerous errors in grammar, mechanics, and spelling.	Sentence structure is poor, affecting the clarity of the writing and making it confusing to the reader; many errors in grammar, mechanics, and spelling.
					_____ / 16

The Hero's Journey

UNIT II
Culminating Essay Prompt

Directions: In this unit, you read about the concept of the *hero's journey*. Why do you think the concept of the *hero's journey* emerged across time and cultures around the world? What message does it bring to society?

Journey Into Conflict

This unit centers on themes related to conflict, as seen through the people, places, and events of the American Revolution and the historical fiction novel *Sophia's War* by Avi. Within the unit, students will read, analyze, evaluate, and interpret the novel, poetry, primary sources, and nonfiction texts, exploring the types of conflict, both personal and societal, experienced during the revolution. They will consider the roles historical figures in the novel played in real life and the 12-year-old protagonist's journey of personal discovery and service to the revolutionary cause, as well as investigate the importance of certain events of the war. Students will demonstrate their growing understanding of this theme through various projects, narrative writing, informational writing, persuasive writing, and poetry.

LESSON 3.1

Setting the Scene: New York During the American Revolution

Common Core State Standards

- W.6.7
- SL.6.1

Materials

- Lesson 3.1 Literature Analysis Model
- Lesson 3.1 Web Scavenger Hunt
- Lesson 3.1 Web Scavenger Hunt: Suggested Resources
- Lesson 3.1 Web Scavenger Hunt: Questions (cut into strips, 3–4 questions per envelope; one envelope per group)
- Student copies of *Sophia's War* by Avi
- Computer and Internet access

Estimated Time

- 60–80 minutes

Objectives

In this lesson, students will:
- conduct a short research task in order to answer questions that build understanding about a topic.

Content

Students will participate in a web search scavenger hunt in order to build background knowledge about the setting of the novel *Sophia's War* by Avi. Students will then share the results of their findings through discussion.

Prior Knowledge

Students will need experience searching for information on the Internet and be able to identify details from a text that support the answer to a research question. Students also need to be familiar with the scavenger hunt format. Students will need to have read through Chapter 10 of *Sophia's War* by Avi.

INSTRUCTIONAL SEQUENCE

1. Have students analyze at least one chapter from *Sophia's War* by Avi using the Literature Analysis Model. For an initial analysis of a chapter, work with students to complete Lesson 3.1 Literature Analysis. You may wish to leave some of the boxes blank that may not be particularly relevant for this type of text. (See pp. 3–4 for additional information about using the Literature Analysis Model.)

2. Assess students' prior knowledge of the American Revolution through a brief discussion. Guiding questions may include:
   - Approximately when was the American Revolution fought?
   - What were some of the events that led up to the revolution?
   - Who governed the people of the 13 colonies?
   - What were some of the important documents related to the revolution?

Teacher's Note. Depending upon your social studies curriculum or students' general background knowledge, clarification of some events of the American Revolution may be necessary. The Kids Discover website has free resources (a free sign-up is required) available that may be useful (http://www.kidsdiscover.com/free-lesson-plans), as does Ducksters (http://www.ducksters.com/history/american_revolution.php).

3. Share with students that they will take part in a web search scavenger hunt to find out more information about the setting and events of *Sophia's War*, set during the time of the American Revolution.

4. Divide students into groups of 3–4 and distribute Lesson 3.1 Web Scavenger Hunt and (optional) Lesson 3.1 Web Scavenger Hunt: Suggested Resources. Provide each group with an envelope containing the questions they are responsible for researching from Lesson 3.1 Web Scavenger Hunt: Questions.

Teacher's Note. Lesson 3.1 Web Scavenger Hunt: Suggested Resources includes a list of possible web resources for students to use as they complete their scavenger hunt. The websites are suggestions identified by the author, and because URLs may be updated or changed, alternative websites may be used at your discretion.

5. Allow 20–30 minutes for students to complete the scavenger hunt. Encourage them to work together and discuss their answers so that each member of the group is familiar with them.

6. When students have completed their search, regroup them using a jigsaw strategy so that there is one student from each of the previous groups in a new group. Allow each new group to share the questions from their scavenger hunts and discuss their findings.

> **Teacher's Note.** Jigsaw is a cooperative learning strategy where students become "experts" on the topic assigned to them and then share their knowledge with other students in a group.
> 1. Divide students into groups of 4–6, and assign each group the topic or questions they will be responsible for answering and learning about.
> 2. Give students time to become familiar with their topic and rehearse the information they will share with the other groups.
> 3. Regroup the students so that there is one "expert" on each topic or set of questions in each new group. Assign one student to be the discussion leader who keeps the conversation on task and makes sure that everyone in the group has a chance to speak.
> 4. Allow each student to present his or her knowledge to the rest of the group.
> 5. Visit each group, listening for the quality of the information shared and making sure that the groups are on task.

7. Facilitate a brief class discussion at the end of this task and ask students to make connections with what they learned in this lesson to what they have read thus far in *Sophia's War*. Guiding questions may include:
   - In Chapter 1, Sophia and her mother witness the hanging of Nathan Hale on their way to New York. Who was Nathan Hale and why did the British hang him?
   - What were the beliefs of the Tories, or loyalists?
   - Why was the document *Common Sense* important and who wrote it?
   - The theme of our unit is *journey into conflict*. What types of conflict has Sophia experienced since returning home to New York?

Extension Activities

Students may:
- create a crossword puzzle using important vocabulary, names, and places related to the American Revolution with at least 10 words across and 10 words down; or
- create a timeline of important events leading up to and including the American Revolution.

LESSON 3.1
Literature Analysis Model

Directions: Complete the Literature Analysis Model about a chapter from *Sophia's War* by Avi.

	Sophia's War: Chapter _____
Key Words	
Important Ideas	
Tone	
Mood	
Imagery	
Symbolism	
Structure of Writing	

Note. Adapted from *Exploring America in the 1950s* (p. 10) by M. Sandling & K. L. Chandler, 2014, Waco, TX: Prufrock Press. Copyright 2014 by Center for Gifted Education. Adapted with permission.

LESSON 3.1
Web Scavenger Hunt

Directions: Your group has received an envelope containing questions for a web scavenger hunt. Write your questions in the appropriate spaces below, and then search the web to find and record the answers to the questions.

Question	Answer	Website Where the Answer Was Found

Challenging Common Core Language Arts Lessons: Grade 5 © Prufrock Press Inc.

Journey Into Conflict

LESSON 3.1

Web Scavenger Hut: Suggested Resources

Directions: The following are suggested web resources to help you gather information for your web scavenger hunt.

1. New York Freedom Trail (http://www.nyfreedom.com)

2. "Revolutionary War" by New York State Parks (http://nysparks.com/historic-preservation/heritage-trails/revolutionary-war/default.aspx)

3. "The American Revolution, 1763–1783" by Library of Congress (http://www.loc.gov/teachers/classroommaterials/presentationsandactivities/presentations/timeline/amrev/north)

4. "American Revolution" by Ducksters (http://www.ducksters.com/history/american_revolution/battle_of_long_island.php)

5. "The American Revolution" by Mr. Nussbaum (http://mrnussbaum.com/american-revolution)

6. "The American Revolutionary War: Keeping Independence" by Social Studies for Kids (http://www.socialstudiesforkids.com/articles/ushistory/revolutionarywar1.htm)

7. "Liberty! The American Revolution" by PBS (http://www.pbs.org/ktca/liberty/chronicle.html)

8. "American Revolution" by History Channel (http://www.history.com/topics/american-revolution)

9. "Thomas Paine's *Common Sense*" by U.S. History (http://www.ushistory.org/us/10f.asp)

LESSON 3.1
Web Scavenger Hunt: Questions

Which state suffered the most human casualties and
death during the American Revolution?

What was the significance of the battle that took place during August
of 1776 in Brooklyn, NY, between the British and Americans?

What were some of the advantages that the British troops had over the Americans?

Why was controlling the Hudson River important to both
the British and the Americans during the war?

Who were the two main groups of soldiers on the
American side during the Revolution?

What were two of the main causes of death of American soldiers during the war?

What was the main reason why soldiers wore uniforms
during the American Revolution?

What was the purpose of the Culper Spy Ring during the American Revolution?

What were some of the main reasons the Americans
fought for independence from British rule?

Who were the "loyalists" and what were their beliefs?

Who were "The Sons of Liberty" and what was their role during the Revolution?

What was the importance of the pamphlet *Common Sense* by Thomas Paine?

LESSON 3.2

Who's Who in the American Revolution?

Common Core State Standards

- RL.6.1
- RL.6.2
- RI.6.1
- W.6.7
- SL.6.1

Materials

- Lesson 3.2 Character Profile
- Lesson 3.2 Historical Figures of the American Revolution (cut into strips, folded, and placed in container)
- Student copies of *Sophia's War* by Avi
- Chart paper with a large, drawn rendition of Lesson 3.2 Character Profile (one per group)
- Markers
- Computer and Internet access

Estimated Time

- 90 minutes

Objectives

In this lesson, students will:
- provide a description of how the central idea of a story is conveyed through particular details.

Content

Students will read and work together to research information about historical figures that are featured in the novel *Sophia's War* in order to understand how they enhance the plot of the story.

Prior Knowledge

Students will need to have read through Chapter 40 of *Sophia's War* by Avi. They will need experience making inferences and explaining them using textual evidence. Students should also be able to work independently to complete a series of short research tasks.

INSTRUCTIONAL SEQUENCE

1. Divide students into groups of 2–4. Distribute Lesson 3.2 Character Profile. Students will work with their group to research facts about the life of one of the historical figures mentioned in *Sophia's War*. They will need to determine how that figure enriches and adds meaning to the story. Some of these people included Nathan Hale, George Washington, Benedict Arnold, Alexander Hamilton, and John André.

2. Ask one student from each group to draw a historical figure from the container (from Lesson 3.2 Historic Figures of the American Revolution). Each group will research facts about the person whose name they have drawn and record their findings on Lesson 3.2 Character Profile. Clarify what each of the sections on the handout means before students begin their research.

3. Afterward, distribute a chart paper rendition of the character profile and markers to each group. Ask them to record as many details from their findings as possible on the chart paper.

4. When each group has recorded their information on their paper, hang the chart paper up around the classroom and conduct a gallery walk, allowing students an opportunity to read about each historical figure.

5. Facilitate a brief classroom discussion about how the addition of real historical figures to a story enriches the plot (makes it more believable, exciting, etc.). In addition, be sure to discuss how each of these figures was involved in the various conflicts of the American Revolution. For example, it was the unreasonable taxes levied on the colonists by King George III that caused rebellions like the Boston Tea Party. Thomas Paine's pamphlet *Common Sense* argued for independence from England and the establishment of a democratic republic, which caused conflict with the British.

Extension Activities

Students may:

- pick a scene from *Sophia's War* and rewrite it to include a real-life revolutionary historical figure that does not appear in the original story and share their rewritten scene with the rest of the class, explaining the choice of character and how they enhanced the story; or
- write a journal entry from the point of view of one of the real historic figures from the novel, connecting it to one of the chapters in the book.

LESSON 3.2
Character Profile

Directions: As you research information about the historical figure assigned to your group, answer the questions in each space with what you have learned about him with a focus on his connection to the American Revolution.

Character's Name: _____

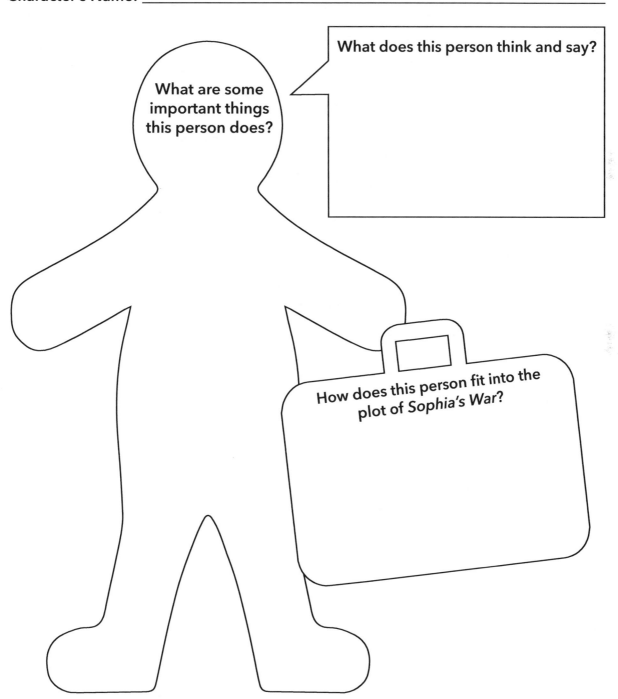

Challenging Common Core Language Arts Lessons: Grade 5 © Prufrock Press Inc.
Permission is granted to photocopy or reproduce this page for single classroom use only.

LESSON 3.2

Historical Figures of the American Revolution

Journey Into Conflict

+---+
| Benedict Arnold |
| |
| Nathan Hale |
| |
| John André |
| |
| George Washington |
| |
| King George III |
| |
| Alexander Hamilton |
| |
| Thomas Paine |
+---+

LESSON 3.3

The Inner and Outer Conflicts Caused by War

Common Core State Standards

- RL.6.1
- RL.6.3
- RL.6.5
- W.6.9

Materials

- Lesson 3.3 Types of Conflict Found in Literature
- Lesson 3.3 Where's the Conflict?
- Lesson 3.3 Story Plot Diagram
- Student copies of *Sophia's War* by Avi
- Large butcher/chart paper with a drawing of a plot diagram (include introduction/exposition, rising action, climax, falling action, and resolution/conclusion)
- Markers or crayons

Estimated Time

- 60 minutes

Objectives

In this lesson, students will:
- cite textual evidence in order to demonstrate understanding of what the text says explicitly as well as inferences drawn from the text.

Content

Students will read and revisit sections of *Sophia's War* by Avi in order to identify the types of literary conflict found in the story, determine where they occur, and how they affect the plot.

> **Teacher's Note.** The learning task in this lesson may be completed over the duration of the unit and used as small-group or independent work. Students may continue to work on their own or with a partner to complete the chart until they reach the end of the book.

Prior Knowledge

Students will need to have completed reading *Sophia's War* or read through Chapter 4 if the learning task will be completed throughout the unit. Students will need experience making inferences and explaining them using textual evidence.

INSTRUCTIONAL SEQUENCE

1. Ask students to talk with a partner about what the word "conflict" means to them. Allow them to share their answers with the rest of the class and clarify if necessary.

2. Explain to students that conflict in the plot of a story helps move it forward and create interest for the reader. Distribute Lesson 3.3 Types of Conflict Found in Literature and briefly review possible types of conflict.

3. Then distribute Lesson 3.3 Where's the Conflict? Choosing an excerpt from the novel, briefly model how to complete the organizer.

4. Allow students to work individually or with a partner to identify and record examples of conflict found in Chapter 3 of *Sophia's War*. For example, students should be able to identify the conflict that occurs between Sophia and her mother at the end of the chapter, when Sophia questions her mother's reasons for lying to the British officer. Move about the classroom to check for understanding and provide assistance if needed.

5. Distribute Lesson 3.3 Story Plot Diagram and display a larger copy of the diagram on butcher/chart paper (see Materials list). Explain that students will record conflicts on the diagram, matching where they occurred in the plot (e.g., during the exposition, climax, resolution, etc.). Using a marker, write down the conflict that students identified in Chapter 3 on the chart paper in the correct place on the diagram (exposition). Have students work on completing their charts and diagrams, either independently or with a partner. Allow small groups to take turns recording their examples of conflicts on the large class diagram as they finish.

6. When all of the types of conflict have been recorded on the story plot diagram, briefly discuss with students about whether they notice any patterns or groupings that stand out in particular. Guiding questions may include:
   - Is there a part of the novel that seems to have more "person versus person" conflicts than other sections?
   - Why does this make sense when considering the plot of the story?
   - Sophia experiences inner conflict throughout the book; what is the cause of most of the inner conflict she experiences? (Her feelings about John André, uncertainty about her role in aiding the efforts of the Patriots in the war.)
   - How does Sophia's conflicting feelings about John André ultimately affect the outcome of the story? (Even though she knows that John André will hang if he is captured, she goes through with her plan to convince the Patriot rebels to intercept him as he attempts to meet with Benedict Arnold.)

Extension Activities

Students may:
   - create a conflict web poster with an image of Sophia in the center and the web elements, illustrating the conflicts she faced that had the most impact on the outcome of the story; or

- choose a scene from the story where Sophia experiences conflict of some kind and rewrite it to reflect a different outcome and predict what might happen next in the story (e.g., in Chapter 45 she takes a letter meant for John André off of his desk to read it, but the scene could be rewritten as if Sophia was too afraid to take the letter off the desk, as a result she does not read it and thus does not immediately find out about the plan to take over West Point).

LESSON 3.3
Types of Conflict Found in Literature

Person Versus Society	A character or group of characters fights against the society in which they live or against social traditions or rules.
Person Versus Self	The character's struggle takes place in his or her own mind, and usually has something to do with making a choice or dealing with mixed feelings and emotions.
Person Versus Person	One character struggles against another character.
Person Versus Nature	A character struggles with some aspect of nature, which could be weather, environment, or animals.

LESSON 3.3
Where's the Conflict?

Directions: Conflict in literature helps to move the plot of a story forward. As you read *Sophia's War* by Avi, write down examples of the types of conflict found in the story, along with a description of each. Be sure to record the chapter and page number where you found the example.

Type of Conflict	Description	Chapter/Page Number

Type of Conflict	Description	Chapter/Page Number

LESSON 3.3
Story Plot Diagram

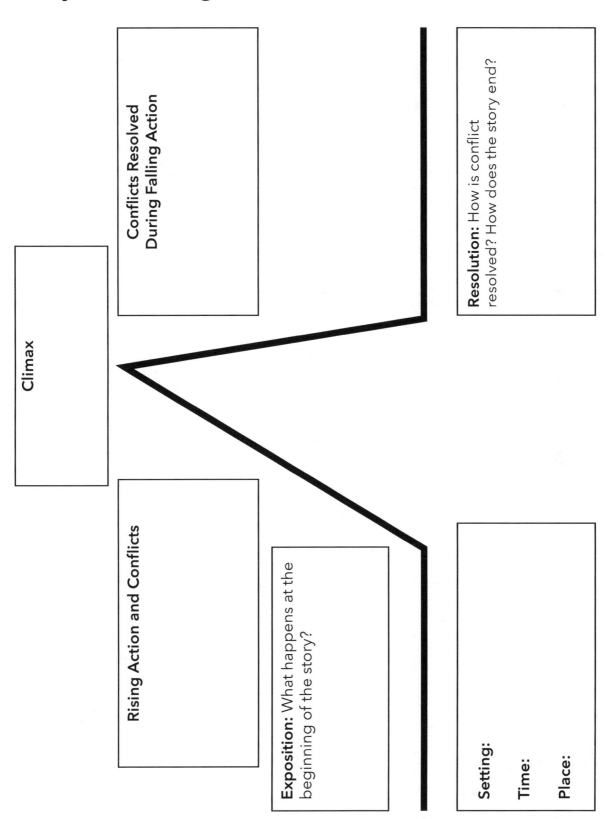

Climax

Conflicts Resolved
During Falling Action

Rising Action and Conflicts

Exposition: What happens at the beginning of the story?

Resolution: How is conflict resolved? How does the story end?

Setting:

Time:

Place:

Journey Into Conflict

LESSON 3.4
Conflicting Reports

Common Core State Standards

- RL.6.1
- RL.6.9
- RI 6.1
- SL.6.1.D

Materials

- Lesson 3.4 How Does It Tell a Story?
- Lesson 3.4 Comparing Literature to History
- Student copies of or access to pages 1–5 of "Letter from Paul Revere to Jeremy Belknap, circa 1798" (http://www.masshist.org/database/viewer.php?item_id=99&img_step=1&mode =transcript#page1)
- Computer and Internet access (optional)

Estimated Time

- 120 minutes

Objectives

In this lesson, students will:
- provide a comparison and contrast of texts in different forms or genres in terms of their approaches to similar themes and topics, and
- determine the theme of a text and how it is conveyed through particular details.

Content

Students will read the poem "Paul Revere's Ride" by Henry Wadsworth Longfellow. They will rewrite the poem in a narrative format in order to interpret the events of the story it tells, then compare it to Paul Revere's own account of what happened the night of April 18, 1775. Students will then discuss some of the reasons why Longfellow's account of Paul Revere's ride, although not entirely accurate, has become a legend in American history.

Prior Knowledge

Students need to know how to compare and contrast texts and the information in them.

INSTRUCTIONAL SEQUENCE

1. As a class, have students share what they know about Paul Revere, one of the better-known figures of the American Revolution. Depending on their background knowledge, they may or may not be familiar with the Henry Wadsworth Longfellow's poem "Paul Revere's Ride," but they may have heard the story associated with it.

2. Distribute Lesson 3.4 How Does It Tell a Story?. Read the poem aloud, as students follow along.

3. Have students read the poem again silently, circling or highlighting any unfamiliar words. Afterward, ask students to talk with a partner about what they think the topic of the poem is.

4. Briefly discuss the poem as a class, pointing out the glossary at the end of the handout. Clarify the meanings of any words that students are still not sure about.

5. Explain to students that they will now "rewrite" each stanza of the poem in the right-hand column of the handout as if they were telling a story. An example is included, but if necessary, model the task using another stanza.

6. When students have completed their story and checked their work, ask a few of the groups to share their story with the class. Clarify or make corrections as necessary.

7. Distribute Lesson 3.4 Comparing Literature to History and copies (or access to) pages 1–5 of "Letter from Paul Revere to Jeremy Belknap, circa 1798."

8. Tell students that they are going to take on the role of historian in order to verify the events in Longfellow's poem about Paul Revere's ride on April 18, 1775. Read pages 1–5 of Revere's letter to Belknap as a class. Students may begin to notice conflicting information in the poem and Revere's letter during the first reading, but encourage them to jot these down on paper rather than reveal them to the class.

9. Ask students to work with a partner to read Revere's letter again and compare it to Longfellow's poem, recording differences they note on the handout. Allow at least 20 minutes for this task. Move about the class to assist students as necessary.

10. When students have completed Lesson 3.4 Comparing Literature to History, ask them to share their answers with the rest of the class.

11. Reveal to the class that Longfellow wrote this poem in 1861, at the beginning of the Civil War. He was deeply concerned about the country's political future, and he wrote the poem as a tribute to a time when freedom was an idea that helped create our nation. In doing so, he took a person who had been relatively forgotten up to that point and made him a national hero, symbolic of bravery, and permanently established him in American culture.

12. As a class, briefly discuss possible reasons why Longfellow made the changes he did to the true story of Revere's ride, and how those changes caused Revere to become a hero in the eyes of the American people. Be sure to include a discussion of how the author's use of figurative and descriptive language adds to the drama of the poem's events. Guiding questions may include:
   - What are some of the differences in the story of Paul Revere's midnight ride that you notice when comparing Longfellow's poem to Paul Revere's letter to Jeremy Belknap?
   - How did the changes Longfellow made to the story of the ride enhance Paul Revere's stature as a hero?
   - Longfellow refers to the British ship the *Somerset* as "A phantom ship, with each mast and spar, Across the moon, like a prison-bar, And a huge, black hulk, that was mag-

nified by its own reflection in the tide." How does the use of descriptive phrases such as "prison-bar," "phantom ship," and "huge black hulk" contribute to the tone of this stanza?

Extension Activities

Students may:

- compose a poem using a completely different structure (such as Haiku, diamante, or cinquain) that retells the essential elements of the story of Paul Revere's ride; or
- conduct research into Longfellow's background to determine the possible reasons why he changed certain elements of the Paul Revere story.

LESSON 3.4
How Does It Tell A Story?

Directions: Read "Paul Revere's Ride" by Henry Wadsworth Longfellow. Then work with a partner to rewrite each section of the poem as if you were telling it as a story. When you are finished, read what you have written to make sure that the "story" flows smoothly and makes sense. The first stanza is done for you. Words in **bold** font appear in a glossary at the end of the poem.

"Paul Revere's Ride" by Henry Wadsworth Longfellow	Stanzas Told in Story Form
Listen, my children, and you shall hear Of the midnight ride of Paul Revere, On the eighteenth of April, in **Seventy-Five**: Hardly a man is now alive Who remembers that famous day and year.	*Boys and girls, listen to the story of Paul Revere's midnight ride. It happened on the night of April 18 in 1775, and hardly anyone who is alive now remembers that famous day and year.*
He said to his friend, "If the British march By land or sea from the town to-night, Hang a lantern aloft in the **belfry**-arch Of the North-Church-tower, as a signal-light,-- One if by land, and two if by sea; And I on the opposite shore will be, Ready to ride and spread the alarm Through every Middlesex village and farm, For the country-folk to be up and to arm."	
Then he said "Good night!" and with muffled oar Silently rowed to the Charlestown shore, Just as the moon rose over the bay, Where swinging wide at her **moorings** lay The Somerset, British **man-of-war**: A phantom ship, with each mast and spar Across the moon, like a prison-bar, And a huge black hulk, that was magnified By its own reflection in the tide.	

"Paul Revere's Ride" by Henry Wadsworth Longfellow	Stanzas Told in Story Form
Meanwhile, his friend, through alley and street Wanders and watches with eager ears, Till in the silence around him he hears The **muster** of men at the barrack door, The sound of arms, and the tramp of feet, And the measured **tread** of the **grenadiers** Marching down to their boats on the shore.	
Then he climbed to the tower of the church, Up the wooden stairs, with stealthy tread, To the belfry-chamber overhead, And startled the pigeons from their perch On the **sombre** rafters, that round him made Masses and moving shapes of shade,-- By the trembling ladder, steep and tall, To the highest window in the wall, Where he paused to listen and look down A moment on the roofs of the town, And the moonlight flowing over all.	
Beneath, in the churchyard, lay the dead, In their night-encampment on the hill, Wrapped in silence so deep and still That he could hear, like a **sentinel's** tread, The watchful night-wind, as it went Creeping along from tent to tent, And seeming to whisper, "All is well!" A moment only he feels the spell Of the place and the hour, and the secret dread Of the lonely belfry and the dead; For suddenly all his thoughts are bent On a shadowy something far away, Where the river widens to meet the bay, -- A line of black, that bends and floats On the rising tide, like a bridge of boats.	

"Paul Revere's Ride" by Henry Wadsworth Longfellow	Stanzas Told in Story Form
Meanwhile, impatient to mount and ride, Booted and spurred, with a heavy stride, On the opposite shore walked Paul Revere. Now he patted his horse's side, Now gazed on the landscape far and near, Then impetuous stamped the earth, And turned and tightened his saddle-girth; But mostly he watched with eager search The belfry-tower of the old North Church, As it rose above the graves on the hill, Lonely and **spectral** and sombre and still. And lo! as he looks, on the belfry's height, A glimmer, and then a gleam of light! He springs to the saddle, the bridle he turns, But lingers and gazes, till full on his sight A second lamp in the belfry burns!	
A hurry of hoofs in a village-street, A shape in the moonlight, a bulk in the dark, And beneath from the pebbles, in passing, a spark Struck out by a steed that flies fearless and **fleet**: That was all! And yet, through the gloom and the light, The fate of a nation was riding that night; And the spark struck out by that steed, in his flight, Kindled the land into flame with its heat.	
He has left the village and mounted the **steep**, And beneath him, tranquil and broad and deep, Is the **Mystic**, meeting the ocean tides; And under the alders, that skirt its edge, Now soft on the sand, now loud on the ledge, Is heard the tramp of his steed as he rides.	

"Paul Revere's Ride" by Henry Wadsworth Longfellow	Stanzas Told in Story Form
It was twelve by the village clock When he crossed the bridge into Medford town. He heard the crowing of the cock, And the barking of the farmer's dog, And felt the damp of the river-fog, That rises when the sun goes down.	
It was one by the village clock, When he galloped into Lexington. He saw the gilded weathercock Swim in the moonlight as he passed, And the meeting-house windows, blank and bare, Gaze at him with a spectral glare, As if they already stood aghast At the bloody work they would look upon.	
It was two by the village clock, When be came to the bridge in Concord town. He heard the bleating of the flock, And the twitter of birds among the trees, And felt the breath of the morning breeze Blowing over the meadows brown. And one was safe and asleep in his bed Who at the bridge would be first to fall, Who that day would be lying dead, Pierced by a British musket-ball.	
You know the rest. In the books you have read, How the British **Regulars** fired and fled,-- How the farmers gave them ball for ball, From behind each fence and farmyard-wall, Chasing the red-coats down the lane, Then crossing the fields to emerge again Under the trees at the turn of the road, And only pausing to fire and load.	

Journey Into Conflict

"Paul Revere's Ride" by Henry Wadsworth Longfellow	Stanzas Told in Story Form
So through the night rode Paul Revere; And so through the night went his cry of alarm To every Middlesex village and farm,-- A cry of defiance, and not of fear, A voice in the darkness, a knock at the door, And a word that shall echo forevermore! For, borne on the night-wind of the Past, Through all our history, to the last, In the hour of darkness and peril and need, The people will waken and listen to hear The hurrying hoof-beats of that steed, And the midnight message of Paul Revere.	

Glossary

Seventy-five: Refers to the year 1775

belfry: A bell tower, usually at the top of a church

moorings: A place where a ship is docked

man-of-war: A war ship

muster: A gathering of soldiers or people

tread: The step of a person walking

grenadiers: A soldier of the guards

somber: Dark and gloomy

sentinel: A guard

spectral: Ghostly; like a phantom

fleet: Moving quickly

steep: A steep or sharp slope

Mystic: A short river that flows into the Boston harbor

Regulars: Soldiers belonging to a permanent, professional army

LESSON 3.4
Comparing Literature to History

Directions: "Paul Revere's Ride" by Henry Wadsworth Longfellow is one of America's most famous poems and has become symbolic of the American Revolution. In fact, during the years following its publication, Longfellow's poem was taken as historical fact. It is your job as a historian to compare the poem to Revere's own account of the story in a letter he wrote in 1798.

"Paul Revere's Ride" by Henry Wadsworth Longfellow	Paul Revere's Ride as Told by Paul Revere

Journey Into Conflict

LESSON 3.5
Reporting the Revolution

Common Core State Standards

- RL.6.1
- RI.6.1
- W.6.2
- W.6.4

Materials

- Lesson 3.5 Hear Ye, Hear Ye! Stories of the Revolution
- Lesson 3.5 Colonial Times Newspaper Template
- Lesson 3.5 Historical Fiction (optional)
- Lesson 3.5 Rubric: Colonial Times Newspaper
- Student copies of *Sophia's War* by Avi
- Computer and Internet access
- Examples of colonial newspapers:
  - *The Maryland Gazette* (http://msa.maryland.gov/msa/stagser/s1259/121/5912/html/0000.html)
  - *The Massachusetts Spy* (http://www.teachushistory.org/node/333)
  - "Early American Newspapering" by James Breig (http://www.history.org/foundation/journal/spring03/journalism.cfm)

Estimated Time

- 90–150 minutes (with additional time set aside for writing and research)

Objectives

In this lesson, students will:
- demonstrate understanding of a theme or central idea of a text and how it is conveyed through particular details by writing to communicate ideas and concepts.

Content

Students will write about a variety of topics related to the novel *Sophia's War* by Avi and the poem "Paul Revere's Ride" by Henry Wadsworth Longfellow and create a colonial-era newspaper.

Prior Knowledge

Students should be familiar with how newspapers are formatted. Students will need to have completed reading *Sophia's War* by Avi and "Paul Revere's Ride" by Henry Wadsworth Longfellow.

INSTRUCTIONAL SEQUENCE

1. As a class, briefly discuss what students have learned about the American Revolution from *Sophia's War*, "Paul Revere's Ride," and researching information about the events and people that were part of the war. Focus on what students learned that surprised them, something that may have changed formerly held beliefs, or something new or interesting. Discuss the fact that even though the war between the colonies and Great Britain was itself an example of conflict, there were many other types of conflicts that led up to the war and were experienced by people who either directly participated in the war or those who experienced the effects of war on their communities.

2. Tell students that one of the only ways that people in the colonies could get news of the war was by reading newspapers. Share a few examples of colonial newspapers (see Materials list). Identify some of their features (contain mostly text; few illustrations, if any; majority of text informs the reader about local, national, and foreign events, etc.).

3. Distribute Lesson 3.5 Hear Ye, Hear Ye! Stories of the Revolution and Lesson 3.5 Colonial Times Newspaper Template. Divide students into groups of 4–5. Explain that they will assume the role of colonial era reporters in order to create a newspaper that relates events concerning the revolution to local readers. Briefly review the requirements, give students an opportunity to decide individual reporter roles, and distribute Lesson 3.5 Rubric: Colonial Times Newspaper.

Teacher's Note. Consider allowing groups to create their newspapers in Microsoft Word, Microsoft Publisher, or other publishing software.

4. If necessary, teach a mini-lesson on the characteristics of the historical fiction genre so that students are able to accurately complete the *Sophia's War* book review portion of the newspaper. Distribute Lesson 2.5 Historical Fiction. Using a book or novel that was previously read by the students, have them identify the characteristics that made it historical fiction. For example, *The Witch of Blackbird Pond* by Elizabeth George Speare takes place in Connecticut in the year 1687 and features characters who are Puritans, as well as detailed descriptions of what life was like in the early colonial days. Included are references to characters that are actual historical figures as well as references to major religious and political debates common to this time period. Other good literary examples include *Johnny Tremain* by Esther Forbes, *Bud, Not Buddy* by Christopher Paul Curtis, and *Crispin: The Cross of Lead* by Avi.

5. When the newspapers are completed and assembled, encourage groups to share their newspapers with others. If the newspapers are completed using publishing software, they may be shared on the school's website or school newspaper.

Extension Activities

Students may:

- create "ads" for their newspaper, by researching local shops, professions, and/or places that might have sponsored a colonial-era newspaper; or
- work with a partner to create an interview between a reporter and a famous figure of the revolution for their newspaper, with one partner creating the interview questions and the other answering them.

LESSON 3.5
Hear Ye, Hear Ye! Stories of the Revolution!

Directions: You have been reading about the American Revolution as told from the perspective of Sophia Calderwood in *Sophia's War* by Avi. One of the few forms of public communication available to people during this time was the newspaper. You and your group will take on the role of 18th-century journalists and research information about the people, places, and events of the American Revolution in order to create a newspaper that informs the colonists about the war.

Members of your group will choose one of the following reporter roles. All roles should be represented in your newspaper.

Famous Battle Reporter

Your job will be to research and report about a famous battle of the American Revolution. Be sure to include the following information:
   a. when and where the battle took place,
   b. important people who were part of the battle, and
   c. what happened during the battle and who won.

Famous People of the War Reporter

Your job is to inform the public about the life and accomplishments of a famous person associated with the Revolution. The person could be a hero, traitor, or spy. Be sure to include the following information:
   a. a short biography of the person's life, such as his or her birthplace, where he or she lived, etc.;
   b. which side of the war he or she supported, the Patriots or the Loyalists/British; and
   c. his or her part in the conflict.

Unfamiliar People of the War Reporter

Your job will be to research and write about a lesser-known person associated with the Revolution. Include some biographical information and his or her role in the Revolution. Choose from one of the groups of people below:
   a. Women
   b. African Americans
   c. American Indians

Important Events Leading to the War Reporter

Your job is to research and describe one of the events that caused conflict between the Americans and the British and ultimately became one of the causes of the American Revolution. Include facts such as who was responsible for or present at the event, what happened, and how it ended. Possible choices may include the following:

a. Boston Tea Party
b. Intolerable Acts
c. Stamp Act
d. Boston Massacre
e. Townshend Act

LESSON 3.5
Colonial Times Newspaper Template

Directions: Use this template as a guide for creating a page for your group's newspaper. Give your newspaper a name, place of publication, and date. When each reporter in the group has finished a page, staple them together to complete the newspaper.

Newspaper Title: _____

Place, Date: _____

Illustration	Article, Column 1	Article, Column 2
Quotes by Famous People of the Revolution		
Mini Review of *Sophia's War* and What Makes it a Work of Historical Fiction		

LESSON 3.4

Historical Fiction

The genre of historical fiction in literature includes stories that are written using a specific time period or historical event as the setting. Here are a few important things to note about the genre.

Setting is an important literary element in historical fiction, and because the author is writing about a particular time in history, it is necessary that the information about the time period be accurate and authentic. The author must research the time period he or she is writing about thoroughly in order to become familiar with how people looked and behaved, what everyday customs were like, and what common tools, clothing, and artifacts they might have used or worn.

Historical fiction usually has characters and settings that are either imaginary or real to the time period. Some of the plot elements may actually have occurred in history, may be fictional, or a combination of both. Even if the setting, plot, and characters are all fictional, the author must portray these in an authentic way in order for the story to be believable.

LESSON 3.5 RUBRIC
Colonial Times Newspaper

	Exceeds Expectations 5 points	Proficient 4 points	Developed 3 points	Emerging 2 points	Novice 1 point
Spelling and Grammar	Spelling and grammar are perfect and require no corrections.	Spelling and grammar have just one or two mistakes.	Spelling and grammar have some mistakes but do not affect the reader's understanding.	Spelling and grammar have numerous mistakes that sometimes affect the reader's understanding.	Spelling and grammar have numerous mistakes throughout and make it difficult for the reader to understand.
Newspaper Components	Contains all of the required components, including four articles, an illustration, quotes by famous people of the war, and a book review of *Sophia's War*. In addition there are additional articles and features, such as an interview or ads.	Contains all of the required components, including four articles, an illustration, quotes by famous people of the war, and a book review of *Sophia's War*.	Contains most of the required components, but is missing an article, an illustration, quotes by famous people of the war, or a book review of *Sophia's War*.	Contains some of the required components, but is missing two of them, either an article, an illustration, quotes by famous people of the war, or the book review of *Sophia's War*.	Contains few of the required components, and is missing three or four of them, either an article, an illustration, quotes by famous people of the war, or the book review of *Sophia's War*.
					_____ / 8

UNIT III
Culminating Essay Prompt

Directions: In this unit, you read *Sophia's War*, a work of historical fiction that blends fictional characters and settings with real ones from the period of the American Revolution. Why do you think it is important for us to learn about past events? Why do you think an author chooses to use a story about a fictional character as a way to teach us about them?

UNIT IV

Journey as a Symbol for Change

This unit centers on the theme of journey as a symbol for change, as related to the Civil Rights Movement. Within the unit, students will read, analyze, evaluate, and interpret nonfiction texts and poetry, examining the content for themes of civil rights, nonviolent protest, and the historical significance of the Montgomery Bus Boycott of 1955–1956 as a catalyst for the movement. They will consider the structural features of informational text, as well as research important civil rights leaders and other events and their roles in the changes that the movement brought about. Students will demonstrate their growing understanding of this theme through various projects, informational writing, persuasive writing, and poetry.

LESSON 4.1
Reasons for the Journey

Common Core State Standards

- W.6.7
- SL.6.1

Materials

- Lesson 4.1 Idea Map
- Lesson 4.1 Note-Taking Organizer
- Lesson 4.1 Brainwriting
- Student copies of *Freedom Walkers* by Russell Freedman
- Computer and Internet access
- Chart paper and markers
- Web resources about Jim Crow laws (optional):
  - "A Brief History of Jim Crow" by Constitutional Rights Foundation (http://www.crf-usa.org/black-history-month/a-brief-history-of-jim-crow)
  - "Segregated America" by Smithsonian National Museum of American History (http://americanhistory.si.edu/brown/history/1-segregated/segregated-america.html)
  - "One Hundred Years of Jim Crow" by America's Black Holocaust Museum (http://abhmuseum.org/category/galleries/one-hundred-years-of-jim-crow)
  - "Civil Rights: Jim Crow Laws" by Ducksters (http://www.ducksters.com/history/civil_rights/jim_crow_laws.php)

Estimated Time

- 60–80 minutes

Objectives

In this lesson, students will:
- cite specific textual evidence to support analysis of primary and secondary sources in order to build understanding about a topic.

Content

Students will research to gather information about the history of Jim Crow laws. Then students will categorize the information to create an in-depth understanding of how the laws affected the rights and freedoms of African Americans and served as a catalyst for the beginning of the Civil Rights Movement.

Prior Knowledge

Students will need to have experience searching for information on the Internet. Students should be able to extract important details from a text in order to gain information about a topic, as well as place information into categories in order to clarify their understanding of a topic. Students will need to have read Chapters 1–3 of *Freedom Walkers* by Russell Freedman.

INSTRUCTIONAL SEQUENCE

1. Distribute Lesson 4.1 Idea Map. Have students briefly look at each of the words and then quickly write down what they know, if anything, about them in each box. Allow 5–7 minutes for this task.

2. Next, allow students a few minutes to share their answers with a partner. When they are finished, ask them to try to think of a word or phrase for the center box that would act as a connecting idea or concept for all of the other words. (Answers for this will vary, but could include the Civil Rights Movement, life in the South for Blacks, Dr. Martin Luther King, Jr., etc.).

3. Display Lesson 4.1 Idea Map, asking students to share some of their answers with the class. Correct any misconceptions as necessary, and discuss the terms that students placed in the center box of the concept map.

4. Tell students that forms of discrimination and segregation were a direct result of Jim Crow laws, which appeared after African Americans won their freedom after the Civil War ended. Jim Crow laws did not interfere with the 13th Amendment to the Constitution, which abolished slavery, but discrimination continued against Blacks and they continued to be treated as second-class citizens by Whites. Explain that the term *Jim Crow laws* could also be placed in the center box of the idea map. Make a connection to what students have read in *Freedom Walkers* so far. Ask: *Under which category would making African Americans sit at the back of the bus be listed?* (Segregation, discrimination.)

5. Have students research the history of Jim Crow laws and their effects on Black society in America (suggested web resources are listed in the Materials section). Distribute Lesson 4.1 Note-Taking Organizer for students to record important ideas and details. Allow students 20–30 minutes for this task.

6. Distribute Lesson 4.1 Brainwriting. Explain to students that this is a written form of the brainstorming process, and will be used to generate categories of important ideas that were gained from their research on the Jim Crow laws. (Brainwriting is a technique credited to German marketing professional Bernd Rohrbach, who published it in in a German sales industry magazine, *Absatzwirtschaft* [Vol. 12, 1969].)

   - Organize students into groups of 3–5. Place an extra copy of Lesson 4.1 Brainwriting in the middle of each group.
   - Ensure that students understand the meaning of each of the categories and how they relate to the center box, the effects of Jim Crow laws on African Americans.
   - Each student will begin by writing an idea in one of the spaces provided. Students then exchange their sheet for one in the middle and write a different idea on the new sheet. The process continues for a few minutes until all of the boxes on the sheets are filled.

7. Next, display Lesson 4.1 Brainwriting and ask students to share their responses and record them in each category. Clarify and make corrections as necessary.

8. Facilitate a brief discussion to summarize student findings, and ask them to think about how they would have *protested* such treatment without resorting to violence. Students will likely share some background knowledge about Dr. Martin Luther King, Jr., and the protest marches he led. Guiding questions may include:

    ▪   How was King able to peacefully protest the treatment of Blacks as a result of the Jim Crow laws?

    ▪   What are some other examples of peaceful protest that you may be familiar with? (People protesting at political rallies, people protesting for things such as higher wages, safer working conditions, or gender equality in the workplace.)

    ▪   What are some of the reasons why peaceful protest is more effective than violent protest?

Extension Activities

Students may:

▪   create a collage of images and words that represent what Mahatma Gandhi was fighting for by using nonviolent protest and how the method inspired Dr. Martin Luther King, Jr.; or

▪   write a poem from the point of view of a person experiencing discrimination as a result of a Jim Crow law and describe how it makes them feel.

LESSON 4.1
Idea Map

Directions: Look at each of the words in the boxes. Quickly write down what you know, if anything, about them in each one. Next, share your answers with the person next to you. When you are finished sharing try and think of a word or phrase for the center box that would act as a connecting idea or concept for all of the other words.

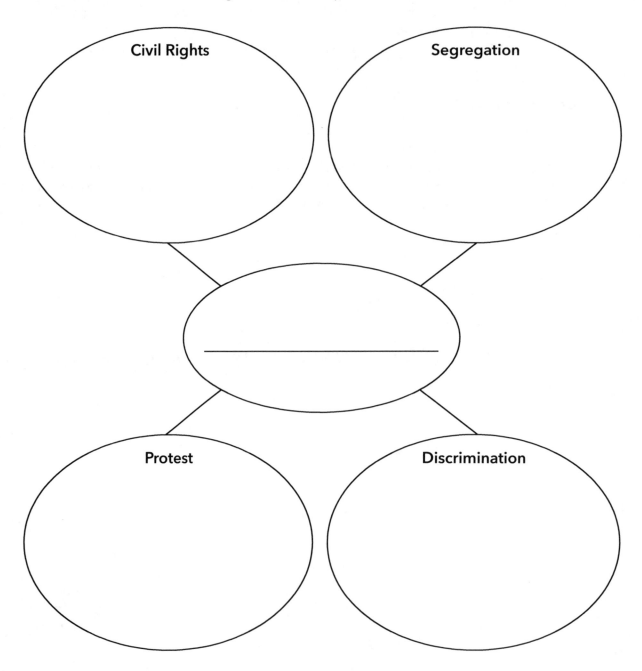

LESSON 4.1
Note-Taking Organizer

Question to Consider	Notes
What was the purpose of Jim Crow laws?	
Why were they called Jim Crow laws? What was the origin of the name?	
What were the "Five Pillars" of Jim Crow laws? How were they designed to oppress Black citizens?	

Journey as Symbol for Change

Question to Consider	Notes
What were some examples of Jim Crow Laws?	
When did Jim Crow Laws end?	
Summary:	

LESSON 4.1
Brainwriting

Directions: Write an idea, word, or phrase related to the subtopic in one of the spaces provided. Next, exchange your sheet for one in the middle of the table and repeat the procedure, this time in another box. Try not to repeat what anyone else has said. Continue this activity until all of the boxes on the sheets are filled.

TOPIC: JIM CROW LAWS

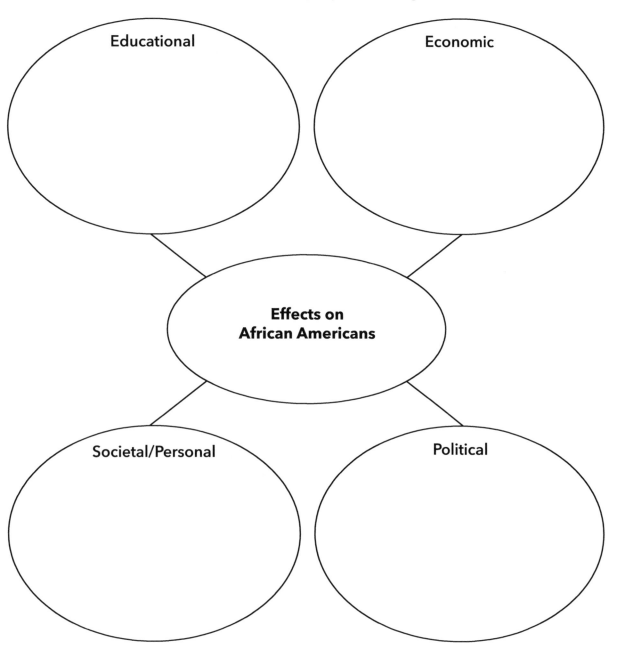

Educational

Economic

Effects on African Americans

Societal/Personal

Political

Journey as Symbol for Change

The Informational Text Highway

Common Core State Standards

- RH.6-8.5
- SL 6.1

Materials

- Lesson 4.2 Literature Analysis Model
- Lesson 4.2 Examples of Text Structures (cut out and placed in envelopes; one envelope per group)
- Lesson 4.2 Text Structures Chart (one per pair)
- Lesson 4.2 Text Structure Organizers
- Student copies of *Freedom Walkers* by Russell Freedman
- Chart paper and markers
- Glue sticks

Estimated Time

- 60–80 minutes

Objectives

In this lesson, students will:
- read and analyze text for organizational structures in order to explain how an author presents information.

Content

Students will review the characteristics and purpose of five different types of text structures by participating in a hands-on matching activity with a partner and then share and justify their answers through a brief class discussion. Next, students will search through the chapters of *Freedom Walkers* that they have read to find examples of each of the text structures and complete a task, which requires them to draw a graphic organizer of the structure and place the example in the organizer to show how the author organized the text.

Prior Knowledge

Students will need to have read through Chapter 6 of *Freedom Walkers* by Russell Freedman. Students should have some prior knowledge of text structures that are found in informational texts.

INSTRUCTIONAL SEQUENCE

1. Have students analyze at least one chapter from *Freedom Walkers* by Russell Freedman, using the Literature Analysis Model. For an initial analysis of a chapter, work with students to complete Lesson 4.2 Literature Analysis Model. You may wish to leave some of the boxes blank that may not be particularly relevant for this type of text. (See pp. 3–4 for additional information about using the Literature Analysis Model.)

2. Divide students into pairs. Explain that when an author writes informational text about a topic, he or she often organizes the information in specific ways so that it is easier for the reader to understand, or to get a specific point across to the reader. Ask students to talk with their partner and make a list of all of the types of text structures they know about.

3. Next, distribute a set of Lesson 4.2 Examples of Text Structures (cut out and placed in envelopes) and Lesson 4.2 Text Structures Chart to each pair.

4. Tell students to work with their partner to place the cut outs of the definitions, clue words, visuals, and examples of each text structure in the correct places on Lesson 4.2 Text Structures Chart. Allow about 10 minutes for this task.

5. When students have finished, ask them to share and justify their thinking. Clarify any misconceptions as necessary, and ask students to make corrections on their sheets.

6. When corrections have been made, students may glue their pieces on Lesson 4.2 Text Structures Chart and use it as a reference for the next part of the lesson.

7. Distribute Lesson 4.2 Text Structures Organizer. Discuss the directions, telling students to read or reread sections of *Freedom Walkers* to find examples of the different types of text structures in order to complete the organizer. It may be necessary to model the task by choosing one of the structures to complete together with the class.

Teacher's Note. It is advisable to begin this task during the lesson to check for student understanding, but then allow students to finish the organizer as they continue to read the book and find examples of other text structures.

8. When students have identified one or two text structures, ask them to write a brief paragraph stating how the structure helped them to understand the author's purpose in using that structure to convey a particular piece of information.

Extension Activities

Students may:

- use their answers from Lesson 2.4 Text Structures Organizer to create a poster on a larger piece of paper that illustrates and explains how text structures organize ideas for readers using the examples from *Freedom Walkers* or another text of their choosing; or

- create an informational pamphlet or brochure that lists all of the text structures and gives examples of each using original text that they have created for this purpose.

LESSON 4.2
Literature Analysis Model

Directions: Complete this Literature Analysis Model about a chapter from *Freedom Walkers* by Russell Freedman.

	Freedom Walkers: Chapter _____
Key Words	
Important Ideas	
Tone	
Mood	
Imagery	
Symbolism	
Structure of Writing	

Note. Adapted from *Exploring America in the 1950s* (p. 10) by M. Sandling & K. L. Chandler, 2014, Waco, TX: Prufrock Press. Copyright 2014 by Center for Gifted Education. Adapted with permission.

Journey as Symbol for Change

NAME:_____ DATE:_____

LESSON 4.2
Examples of Text Structures

Structure	Definition	Visual	Clues	Example
Description	Several details that describe something in order to give the reader a mental picture.		Lots of adjectives, characteristics and examples of the topic being discussed.	*The chocolate cake had a vanilla frosting that was creamy, white, and smooth. The taste was sweet and delicious!*
Cause and Effect	A description of an event or events that are the cause of something followed by a description of the effects.		*As a result, the cause is, due to, because of, the reason is, a possible effect.*	*Molly forgot to add baking powder to the cake recipe. As a result, the cake did not rise while baking and was very flat.*
Sequence/ Chronological Order	A list of events that happen in order or steps to a procedure.		Order words, events told in sequence, *first, next, then, finally,* step-by-step directions.	*First, Molly creamed together the sugar and butter. Next, she added the eggs. Finally, she added all of the dry ingredients.*
Problem and Solution	Information about a problem is presented followed by explanations of one or more solutions.		*One problem is, an issue, a solution, a possible solution, causes a problem, a good idea is to, a difficulty might be.*	*When it was time to add milk to the cake recipe, Molly discovered she did not have enough. She solved the problem by adding a little cream to the milk.*

Journey as Symbol for Change

Structure	Definition	Visual	Clues	Example
Compare and Contrast	A description of the similarities and differences between living things, objects, concepts or ideas.		Similar to, on one hand, in contrast, the difference is, on the other hand, as opposed to, unlike, instead of, however.	*Molly tried both the chocolate cake and the carrot cake. Both cakes were moist and delicious, however there was more frosting on the chocolate cake.*

Challenging Common Core Language Arts Lessons: Grade 5 © Prufrock Press Inc.

Permission is granted to photocopy or reproduce this page for single classroom use only.

121

LESSON 4.2
Text Structures Chart

Directions: Work with a partner to place the cut pieces of the definition, clue words, visual, and example of each text structure type onto the correct place on this organizer. When the class has shared answers, make any necessary corrections, then glue the pieces down in place.

Structure	Definition	Visual	Clues	Example
Description				
Cause and Effect				

Journey as Symbol for Change

Structure	Definition	Visual	Clues	Example
Sequence/ Chronological Order				
Problem and Solution				
Compare and Contrast				

LESSON 4.2
Text Structures Organizer

Directions: As you read through chapters in *Freedom Walkers* by Russell Freedman, find examples of the following text structures. In the spaces below, draw the graphic organizer that matches the text structure. Next, rewrite the information from the text inside the graphic organizer. Think about how the use of the structure helped you to better understand the author's purpose.

Structure	Organizer
Description	
Cause and Effect	

Journey as Symbol for Change

Structure	Organizer
Sequence/ Chronological Order	
Problem and Solution	
Compare and Contrast	

LESSON 4.3
Voices Against Oppression

Common Core State Standards

- RL.6.1
- RL.6.2
- W.6.3.D
- SL.6.1

Materials

- Lesson 4.2 Shared Inquiry Discussion Partner Evaluation
- Lesson 4.2 Rubric: Poem
- Teacher and students copies of or access to "I, Too," "Go Slow," "Democracy," and "As I Grew Older" by Langston Hughes
- Computer and Internet access (optional)
- Clipboards for discussion (optional)
- Teacher's resources:
  - "Langston Hughes Biography" by Scholastic (http://www.scholastic.com/teachers/contributor/langston-hughes)
  - "Langston Hughes" by PBS Kids (http://www.pbs.org/wnet/newyork//laic/episode5/topic2/e5_t2_s3-lh.html)
  - "Shared Inquiry Handbook" by The Great Books Foundation (http://www.greatbooks.org/wp-content/uploads/2014/12/Shared-Inquiry-Handbook.pdf)

Estimated Time

- 60–120 minutes (with additional time set aside for discussion and writing)

Objectives

In this lesson, students will:
- demonstrate their understanding of a theme or central idea of a text and how it is conveyed through particular details by participating in discussions and writing to convey a related message.

Content

Students will read four poems by Langston Hughes and analyze them to determine how the poet communicates theme through word choice. They will examine the author's use of metaphor and symbolism and participate in a shared inquiry in order to discuss the thematic content of the poems and their connection to content they have learned while reading *Freedom Walkers*. Finally, students will use the events surrounding the Montgomery Bus Boycott to create a poem of their own, either using the jazz style format of Langston Hughes or another structure of their choosing.

Prior Knowledge

Students should have some knowledge of figurative language. Students will need to have completed reading *Freedom Walkers* by Russell Freedman. Students should have had prior experience writing poetry. Students should have experience with shared inquiry discussions.

INSTRUCTIONAL SEQUENCE

1. Briefly share some biographical information about Langston Hughes with students. You may refer to the websites mentioned in the materials section of this lesson, or share one of several short videos available about him on TeacherTube and YouTube. Tell students that as a writer, Hughes wanted to highlight the concerns and challenges faced by the Black community in America during his lifetime, which also overlapped with the Civil Rights Movement.

2. Display copies of "I, Too," "Go Slow," "Democracy," and "As I Grew Older" by Langston Hughes. Read each poem aloud to the class, paying careful attention to phrasing and timing between each stanza. Ask students if they can detect a common theme among all four poems. At this point, students should be able to notice that the speaker in each poem talks about injustice and the desire for equality.

3. Starting with "Go Slow," and using a think-aloud strategy, model analyzing elements of the poem to determine the overall meaning. For example, the first three lines of the poem read "Go slow, they say- /while the bite of the dog is fast." Who is the dog (the White man)? Why did Hughes pick a dog to symbolize the White man? Why are certain words italicized? Is the line *"Don't Demonstrate! Wait!-"* meant for the Black man? In addition to modeling the think-aloud strategy, model the use of written annotations that highlight specific word choice or ask questions about parts of the text. Continue this process until you have discussed an interpretation of the poem with students. (A person, presumably African American, is expressing frustration at being told to "go slow" in terms of demanding equal rights and wonders why he must forgive the White man.)

4. Next, reread the poem "I, Too." This time, work together with students to determine the theme of the poem and how Hughes conveys ideas through metaphor (sitting at the table when company comes) and use of language ("I, too, sing America," "I, too, am America"). Guiding questions may include:
    *   The first stanza refers to "the darker brother" (the Black man) being sent to the kitchen to eat when company comes. What do you think the man means when he says "But I laugh, /And eat well, /And grow strong."?
    *   What do you think being "at the table" represents in the poem? (Equality.)
    *   After reading the poem, what could be the meaning of the first and last lines, "I, too, sing America" and "I, too, am America"? (Perhaps the man in the poem "sings" the praises of America and in hoping for a future where he is considered equal to the White man he declares that he, too is part of America.)

5. Facilitate a brief discussion about the message in the poems and their connection to what students have read about the people in *Freedom Walkers*. For example, in "Go Slow," the

speaker in the poem expresses frustration at the fact that he must wait to be treated with equality. The tone of "I, Too" is more hopeful, with the speaker expressing confidence that there will be a day when he will be seated at the same "table" as the White man. Reference the Rosa Parks quote "The only tired I was, was tired of giving in." Ask: *How does that quote relate to "Go Slow" and "I, Too"?*

6. Divide students into pairs. Tell them that they will reread the poems "Democracy" and "As I Grew Older." Working with their partner, they will analyze each poem for meaning, the author's use of figurative language, and connections to *Freedom Walkers*. Encourage them to annotate the text of both poems as they work and to write down any questions they might have that are directly related to the text.

7. When students have finished reading and annotating the poems, tell them that they will participate in a shared inquiry discussion focused on the two poems they have read and analyzed during this lesson.

8. If students have no prior experience with shared inquiry, briefly explain this strategy and the types of questions associated with it (factual, interpretive, evaluative) to the class. Reference the Great Books Foundation website (listed in the Materials section) for an explanation of the shared inquiry format. With students who have never participated in a shared inquiry discussion, it would be advisable to have the teacher act as discussion leader and create the questions. However, if students have had experience, it would be preferable to select a student to act as discussion leader for the group.

9. Explain to students that the class will conduct a shared inquiry discussion using a fishbowl strategy. The class will be divided into two groups and each group will analyze one of the poems. This will allow more students to get a chance to enter the discussion. Rearrange seating into an inner and outer circle. Make sure that students have their annotated copies of "Democracy" and "As I Grew Older."

10. Distribute Lesson 4.3 Shared Inquiry Discussion Partner Evaluation. Explain to students that while the inner group participates in the shared inquiry discussion about the first poem, a partner from the outer group will listen, observe, and note the quality of their participation. The roles will switch when the discussion moves from the first poem to the second. The partner evaluation holds every student accountable for participation in the discussion, as well as giving the group observing a purposeful task while listening to the discussion.

11. Choose one of the two poems as the topic for discussion.
    - Begin with asking students a factual question that ensures comprehension: *What does the word* democracy *mean?*
    - An interpretive question might be: *What does the speaker in the poem mean when he says "I do not need my freedom when I'm dead. I cannot live on tomorrow's bread"?*
    - Evaluative questions ask students to make judgments about whether what the author has written about is true according to our own experiences: *Do you agree that it is important to actively pursue freedom and equality for oppressed populations as opposed to just waiting for it to happen on its own?*

12. After asking examples of all three types of questions, allow approximately 20 minutes before switching groups and repeating the process with the remaining poem. Make sure to include questions that not only address the thematic content of each poem, but also ones that address Hughes's use of poetic devices such as repetition, symbolism, and metaphor. ("Democracy" speaks to the need for actively pursuing equal rights, and "As I Grew Older"

is a comment on the negative effects of racism and how one should make a stand against an unjust society.)

13. Afterward, allow students 5 minutes to talk to their partner and share their partner evaluations.

14. Tell students that they will write their own poem based on the theme of civil rights and the events recounted in *Freedom Walkers*. They may write in the style of Hughes. Literary devices Langston Hughes used often included repetition, rhyme, metaphor, simile, and symbolism. They may also choose a different format, such as diamante, free verse, or acrostic. The goal is for students to take their understanding of the ideas and concepts found in *Freedom Riders* and communicate them through the compact language of poetic form. Distribute Lesson 4.3 Rubric: Poem before students begin.

Extension Activities

Students may:

- schedule a "café" poetry reading where students invite their parents, serve refreshments, and have an opportunity to read and perform their poems out loud; or
- create an interpretive dance to accompany a reading of their poem.

LESSON 4.3
Shared Inquiry Discussion Partner Evaluation

Directions: Complete the following questions based on your partner's contributions to the discussion.

Peer's Name: _____ **Title of Text:** _____

Record a tally mark below for each time your partner contributed in a meaningful way.

On a scale of 1–5, with 5 being the highest, how well did your partner do at the following:

1. _____ **Analysis and reasoning.** Think about these points when you evaluate your partner's discussion. Did your partner:
   a. give reasons and evidence for statements with support from the text?
   b. demonstrate that he or she had given thought and consideration to the topic?
   c. provide relevant and insightful comments?

   Notes/Comments:

2. _____ **Discussion skills.** Did your partner:
   a. speak loudly and clearly?
   b. stay on topic?
   c. stay focused on the discussion?
   d. share talk-time equally with others?

   Notes/Comments:

3. _____ **Civility.** Did your partner:
   a. listen to others respectfully?
   b. enter the discussion in a polite manner?

   Notes/Comments:

Journey as Symbol for Change

LESSON 4.3 RUBRIC

Poem

Journey as Symbol for Change

	Exceeds Expectations 5 points	Proficient 4 points	Developed 3 points	Emerging 2 points	Novice 1 point
Organization and Theme/ Message	Conveys a message/theme that is very appropriate to the topic; enables the reader to reflect upon the topic in new and different ways; is an outstanding example of the chosen poetry format.	Conveys a message/theme that is very appropriate to the topic; enables the reader to reflect upon the topic in new and different ways; is an excellent example of the chosen poetry format.	Conveys a message/theme that is appropriate to the topic; enables the reader to reflect upon the topic; is a good example of the chosen poetry format.	Conveys a message/theme that is somewhat appropriate to the topic; enables the reader to reflect upon the topic; is a fair example of the chosen poetry format.	Conveys a message/theme that has little connection to the topic; does not enable the reader to make additional connections to the topic; is a poor example of the chosen poetry format.
Elements of Poetry	Uses a wide variety of sensory details and figurative language that contribute significantly to the meaning of the poem; effectively uses sound devices such as rhyme, onomatopoeia, and alliteration, as well as vivid word choice to enhance the mood or tone.	Uses a variety of sensory details and figurative language that contribute to the meaning of the poem; effectively uses sound devices such as rhyme, onomatopoeia, and alliteration, as well as vivid word choice to enhance the mood or tone.	Uses some sensory detail and figurative language that contributes to the meaning of the poem; effectively uses some sound devices such as rhyme, onomatopoeia, and alliteration, as well as some vivid word choice to enhance the mood or tone.	Uses little sensory detail and figurative language in the poem; uses one or two sound devices such as rhyme, onomatopoeia, and alliteration, as well as some vivid word choice to enhance the mood or tone.	Uses almost no sensory detail and figurative language that could contribute to the meaning of the poem; uses almost no sound devices such as rhyme, onomatopoeia, and alliteration, as well as no vivid word choice.
Mechanics and Spelling	No errors in mechanics or spelling.	Very few errors in mechanics or spelling.	Some errors in mechanics or spelling.	Errors in mechanics or spelling that sometimes make it difficult to understand the poem.	Many errors in mechanics or spelling that make it very difficult to understand the poem.
					_____ / 12

LESSON 4.4

Journey Through the Civil Rights Movement

Common Core State Standards

- RH.6-8.1
- RI.6.7
- SL.6.1

Materials

- Lesson 4.4 Creating An Artifact Box
- Lesson 4.4 Artifact Box Research Topics
- Lesson 4.4 Artifact Box Research Tool
- Lesson 4.4 Rubric: Artifact Box
- Computer and Internet access
- A shoebox or something similar for each group to use as an artifact box
- Various craft supplies, such as scraps of wood, cloth, Styrofoam, clay, craft sticks, markers, glue, paint, scissors, etc.

Estimated Time

- 60–120 minutes (with additional time set aside for research)

Objectives

In this lesson, students will:
- integrate knowledge and information gathered from primary and secondary resources with visual media in order to communicate a coherent understanding of a topic.

Content

Students will work in groups to conduct research about a person or event associated with the Civil Rights Movement. Based on their research, they will work together to determine how they will represent that person or event using artifacts. Students will then create the artifacts and place them in a box that they have altered or decorated to reflect the contents. They will share their artifact boxes with the rest of the class in a gallery walk.

INSTRUCTIONAL SEQUENCE

1. Display the following quote by Dr. Martin Luther King, Jr.:

   Justice and equality, I saw, would never come while segregation remained, because the basic purpose of segregation was to perpetuate injustice and inequality.

Ask students to turn and talk about what the quote means and its context within the events of the Montgomery Bus Boycott. If necessary, have students reread pages 54–55.

2. Ask students to share their answers and facilitate a brief discussion about how King realized that the only way to gain full equality for Black citizens was to eliminate the practice of segregation in society. The Montgomery Bus Boycott was important because it acted as a catalyst for this, as well as the rest of the Civil Rights Movement. The length of the boycott drew national attention to the cause and people around the country were made aware of King and his position of leadership within the national movement. It also demonstrated that the nonviolent method of protest was effective.

3. Divide students into groups of four. Distribute Lesson 4.4 Creating An Artifact Box, Lesson 4.4 Artifact Box Research Topics, Lesson 4.4 Artifact Box Research Tool, and Lesson 4.4 Rubric: Artifact Box. Briefly discuss the project with students, telling them that they will select a person or event closely associated with the Civil Rights Movement, conduct research about that person or event in order to complete the Artifact Box Research Tool, and then decide upon artifacts to create that best represent the most important characteristics of their topic.

Teacher's Note. If possible, provide a model artifact box based on a person or event from another era in history. An artifact box about the sinking of the Titanic may include items such as sample menus; a pocket watch; boarding tickets for first, second, or third class; a model iceberg; model signage from the ship; an "SOS" in Morse code; or letters from passengers.

4. Allow groups an opportunity to read over the topics. Each group should decide on a topic and how to divide the research tasks and then begin their research based on the requirements of the research tool.

5. Encourage students to revisit some of the websites they have used in earlier lessons, as well as books from their school or home library. Allow adequate time for research. Students should keep track of sources and include them in a bibliography to be turned in with the artifact box.

6. When students have completed their research, they should brainstorm to determine the kinds of artifacts they will create and the materials they will need to work with. They should ask themselves "What makes the person/event unique? How would we represent the knowledge we have about the person/event with an artifact?"

7. Give students 3–4 class periods to complete the artifact box. When the boxes are complete, arrange them around the room museum-style and have each group share its product with the rest of the class. This would also be an excellent opportunity to invite other classes to see the project. Each group would then sit with the artifact box it created and explain the meaning behind each artifact to visiting students and teachers.

Teacher's Note. Consider writing a letter home to parents informing them of the project and adding a request for any extra materials that the school does not have available.

Extension Activities

Students may:

- assume the role of historian and use a web tool such as Prezi (http://prezi.com), Animoto (https://animoto.com), or Nearpod (https://nearpod.com) to create a narrated presentation that tells the story of the artifacts and how they are related to the event or person portrayed; or

- write a journal or diary to accompany the artifacts from the point of view of one of the persons who may have experienced the event or the actual person represented by the artifacts.

LESSON 4.4
Creating an Artifact Box

Directions: What is an artifact, exactly? An *artifact* is an object produced or crafted by humans that can be a tool, ornament, or some object of historical interest. For this assignment, you will choose a person or event closely associated with the Civil Rights Movement and produce an artifact box containing at least eight artifacts that your group has created that reflect your learning about that person or event. Follow each step below.

Step 1: Research Questions

As a team, you will use research questions to help guide your research. The objects and materials in your artifact box must reflect evidence of your research and must make a clear connection to the person or event you have chosen. A copy of each team member's research notes will be collected.

Step 2: Reference List

Each team member must turn in a list of references used to complete the research on the project due date in the form of a bibliography.

Step 3: Creating the Artifact Box

Your team must create a minimum of eight artifacts that reflect your research on a person or event of the Civil Rights Movement. Artifacts must be student-created and have a tag that explains in writing what the artifact represents. No store-bought or electronic items are allowed! Decorate your artifact box to reflect concepts related to the Civil Rights Movement. Work together with your team to brainstorm ideas for artifacts and equally divide the tasks. Supplies will be available for your use but you are welcome to bring in your own.

Step 4: Presentation

When your group has completed the artifact box, you will present a 5-7 minute explanation of your project to the class. Your presentation should be organized and each group member should speak about the artifacts he or she created.

LESSON 4.4
Artifact Box Research Topics

Directions: Together with your group, review this list of people and events related to the Civil Rights Movement. Choose one person or event to research and use as a subject for your artifact box. Can you think of any others that are not on this list?

People	Events
Rosa Parks	Montgomery Bus Boycott
Dr. Martin Luther King, Jr.	*Brown vs. the Board of Education of Topeka*
Marian Anderson	Freedom Rides of 1961
Ralph Abernathy	March on Washington, 1963
Thurgood Marshall	Voting Rights Act of 1965
Medgar Evers	Selma to Montgomery March of 1965
Roy Wilkins	Lunch Counter Sit-Ins, 1960
Shirley Chisholm	Civil Rights Act of 1964
Dorothy Height	Little Rock Nine

Journey as Symbol for Change

LESSON 4.4
Artifact Box Research Tool

Directions: Use the questions below to help focus your research. As you find the answers to your research questions, be sure to record the sources you used for inclusion in your bibliography.

Question	Notes	Sources
How was the person/ event related to the Civil Rights Movement? Provide some biographical/ background information.		
How did this person/ event directly affect the Civil Rights Movement?		

Journey as Symbol for Change

Question	Notes	Sources
What was the major goal of the person/event? Was it accomplished?		
Who were other people who helped or were involved with the person/event and their role in the Civil Rights Movement?		
How did the person/event demonstrate nonviolent protest?		

LESSON 4.4 RUBRIC

Artifact Box

Journey as Symbol for Change

	Exceeds Expectations 5 points	Proficient 4 points	Developed 3 points	Emerging 2 points	Novice 1 point
Connection to Content	Shows outstanding connections to content, covering the most important facts and details of the event or person's life, with additional connections to other people and events.	Shows excellent connections to content, covering the most important facts and details of the event or person's life.	Shows good connections to content, covering many important facts and details of the event or person's life,	Shows some connections to content, but some of the most important facts and details of the event or person's life are missing.	Shows very few connections to content, with many facts and details of the event or person's life missing.
Evidence of Research and Knowledge	Outstanding evidence of research and depth of content knowledge, with a wide variety of sources referenced.	Excellent evidence of research and depth of content knowledge, with a wide variety of sources referenced.	Good evidence of research and depth of content knowledge, with a variety of sources referenced.	Some evidence of research and content knowledge, with a few sources referenced.	Little evidence of research and content knowledge, with few sources referenced.
Writing and Detail	Outstanding use of the conventions of spelling, punctuation, and grammar, with no mistakes and outstanding use of descriptive language.	Excellent use of the conventions of spelling, punctuation, and grammar, with almost no mistakes and excellent use of descriptive language.	Good use of the conventions of spelling, punctuation, and grammar, with 5–10 mistakes and some good examples of descriptive language.	Fair use of the conventions of spelling, punctuation, and grammar, with 10–15 mistakes and a few examples of descriptive language.	Poor use of the conventions of spelling, punctuation, and grammar, with more than 15 mistakes and almost no use of descriptive language.
Bibliography	Has more than 10 sources, all properly cited.	Has 8–10 sources, all properly cited.	Has 5–8 sources, almost all properly cited.	Has 3–5 sources, with only some properly cited.	Has 1–3 sources, with most not properly cited.
					_____ / 16

UNIT IV
Culminating Essay Prompt

Directions: In this unit, you learned about the people and events of the Civil Rights Movement. How were the journeys people made during the Montgomery Bus Boycott, whether walking miles to work or marching in protest against injustice, a symbol for change in the Civil Rights Movement in America?

Journey as Symbol for Change

ANSWER KEY

Lesson 1.2 Notes Organizer

Sample answers are in bold.

Name of Explorer: **Ernest Shackleton**	Group Name: **The Bank of London**
Source: ***Shipwreck at the Bottom of the World**, **Chapter 1, "The Imperial Trans-Antarctic Expedition," pp. 4–5**	
Research Question: What were some of the personal beliefs or character traits of the expedition leaders that affected the outcome of the expedition in some way?	Notes (Answers to the Research Question): **Page 4: Although Shackleton regretted not being the first to get to the South Pole, he decided on a new goal of crossing the continent of Antarctica from side to side.** **Page 5: Shackleton felt that the only thing he was good at was being an explorer.** **Page 5: "the continent pulled him like a magnet"; this probably means that Shackleton had a really strong desire to explore the Antarctic.** **Page 5: As a child, Shackleton dreamed of becoming famous and making lots of money.** **Page 5: Shackleton was very good at raising money for his expeditions, and he was smart enough to think ahead in planning for how he would make money from the photographs and diaries of the crew.**
Summary: **Shackleton decided that exploring the Antarctic was something he really wanted to do, and he persevered in gathering enough money to make it happen. By planning for how he would profit from the expedition before he even started the journey, it seems that he was determined to be successful from the beginning.**	

Lesson 1.4 Investigating Infographics

Sample answers are in bold.

Title: **Healthy Snacks: Why We Need Them**	
Topic	**This infographic informs the reader about why snacks can be good for you, and why it is important to eat snacks that are healthy.**
Facts	**The infographic tells the reader how snacks can give you energy. There is information about why snacks with a lot of sugar are not good for you.**
Elements That Support Understanding	**Data charts; illustrations of healthy and nonhealthy snacks.**
Attention Grabbers	**Simple, bold fonts; interesting, "wow" facts about the effects of unhealthy snacks.**
Colors and Graphics	**Three, bold, contrasting colors; simple, uncomplicated graphics.**

Lesson 2.1 Hero Concept Organizer

Sample answers are in bold.

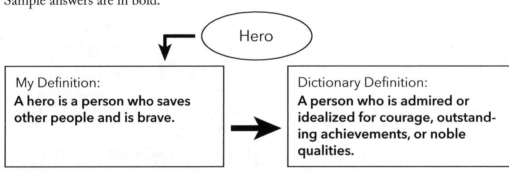

Hero

My Definition:
A hero is a person who saves other people and is brave.

Dictionary Definition:
A person who is admired or idealized for courage, outstanding achievements, or noble qualities.

Heroes You Have Read About in Literature:
Harry Potter, Hercules, Charlotte Doyle, Frodo

Example:	People You Think Are Heroes:	Related Words/Phrases:
Superman **A fireman** **A policeman**	**Dr. Martin Luther King, Jr.** **Harriet Tubman** **My mom and dad**	**Brave** **Strong** **Fearless** **Cares about others**
Nonexample: **A person who is a coward.**		

A Sentence Using the Word *Hero*:
The lifeguard who saved the drowning girl was declared a hero by her parents.

Lesson 2.1 Journey Concept Organizer

Sample answers are in bold.

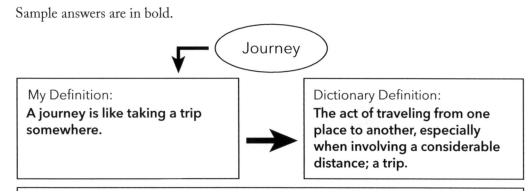

My Definition:	Dictionary Definition:
A journey is like taking a trip somewhere.	**The act of traveling from one place to another, especially when involving a considerable distance; a trip.**

Journeys You Have Read About in Literature:
Professor Sherman's journey in *The Twenty-One Balloons*, Ernest Shackleton's trip to the Antarctic in *Shipwreck at the Bottom of the World*.

Example: **Taking a trip from the East Coast to the West Coast of the U.S.**	Types of Journeys You Know About: **Going on a camping trip with my family.** **Going on a field trip with my class.** **Taking a trip on a plane to see my grandparents.**	Related Words/Phrases: **Voyage** **Expedition** **Tour** **Flight**
Nonexample: **Staying at home.**		

A Sentence Using the Word *Journey*:
This summer my parents took us on a journey to Yellowstone National Park.

Lesson 2.2 Myths and the Hero's Journey

Answers are in bold.

Questions	Textual Evidence
Who is the hero in this story? What are the hero's character traits?	**Answers will vary depending upon the myth students read. Theseus/Jason.**
Does the hero go on a journey? What are some of the challenges the hero faces along the way?	**Answers will vary depending upon the myth students read. Theseus goes on a journey to the island of Crete in order to kill the Minotaur, a monster that is half bull, half man. After he kills the monster he must try to escape back out of a labyrinth. Jason goes on a journey to retrieve the Golden Fleece from the island of Colchis so that he can return it to King Pelias and reclaim his rightful throne.**
Does the hero have someone to help him? If so, describe who that person is and how he or she provides help.	**Answers will vary depending upon the myth students read. Ariadne, the daughter of King Minos, helps Theseus by giving him a thread so that he can retrace his steps back out of the Labyrinth. Medea, the daughter of King Aeëtes's daughter is the person who helps Jason with completing the three tasks required of him in order to obtain the fleece.**

Questions	Textual Evidence
Does the hero face a major obstacle during his journey? Describe what it is and whether or not the hero was able to overcome it.	**Answers will vary depending upon the myth students read. The major obstacle for Theseus is the Minotaur. Jason faces numerous obstacles on the voyage by sea to Colchis, in addition to having to fight the dragon that protects the Golden Fleece. Both heroes overcome all obstacles placed in their path.**
Does the hero return home from the journey? Does anyone help him to do this, and if so, how do they provide assistance?	**Answers will vary depending upon the myth students read. Theseus successfully returns home from the journey, but forgets to replace the black sails on his ship with white ones, which would have notified his father that all was well. Instead, his father sees the black sails and kills himself. Jason returns home to King Pelias with the Golden Fleece, ready to claim his throne.**
Describe what you think the hero has learned from his experiences on the journey.	**Answers will vary depending upon the myth students read. Perhaps Theseus learned a hard lesson about being forgetful, since his father unnecessarily killed himself because he thought his son was dead when he saw the black sails. Jason encountered many trials and challenges on his journey; he probably learned the value of perseverance, since he had to complete the tasks required by the king of Colchis in order to obtain the fleece.**

Lesson 3.3 Where's the Conflict?

Sample answers are in bold.

Type of Conflict	Description	Chapter/Page Number
Person Versus Self	**Sophia is conflicted about her feelings for John André when he charms her with his attention even when she knows he is the enemy.**	**Chapter 12**
Person Versus Nature	**Sophia has to face trekking through the woods by herself and crossing the Hudson River to get to West Point and warn Colonel Livingston about John André's betrayal. She is afraid of wild animals and does not have the proper clothes or shoes for such a journey.**	**Chapters 54–55**
Person Versus Person	**Sophia tries to convince Colonel Livingston that the British are going to send a ship to spy on West Point. He does not want to believe her because she is a young girl.**	**Chapter 58**
Person Versus Society	**Sophia is surrounded by loyalists when she is employed at the Kings Crown. She feels strongly about the injustices done to the colonists by the British and doesn't understand how the other women she works with would not feel the same way.**	**Chapter 41**

REFERENCES

Baskin, B. H., & Harris, K. H. (1980). *Books for the gifted child.* New York, NY: Bowker.

Center for Gifted Education. (2011). *Guide to teaching language arts for high-ability students.* Dubuque, IA: Kendall Hunt.

Harvey, S., & Goudvis, A. (2007). *Strategies that work: Teaching comprehension for understanding and engagement.* Portland, ME: Stenhouse.

McKeague, P. M. (2009). *Writing about literature: Step by step.* Dubuque, IA: Kendall Hunt.

National Governors Association Center for Best Practices, & Council of Chief State School Officers. (2010). *Common Core State Standards for English language arts.* Washington, DC: Authors.

Sandling, M., & Chandler, K. L. (2014). *Exploring America in the 1950s.* Waco, TX: Prufrock Press.

ABOUT THE AUTHOR

Magdalena Fitzsimmons is a S.T.A.T. (Students and Teachers Accessing Tomorrow) resource teacher at the George Washington Carver Center for Arts and Technology, Baltimore County Public Schools in Baltimore, MD. She is a graduate of the Peabody Institute of Johns Hopkins University, City University of New York, Brooklyn College, and the University of Calgary, Canada. Magdalena has presented at numerous national and state conferences on the topics of arts integration, problem-based learning, curriculum for gifted students, creativity, and technology integration. She has also written and edited reading language arts curriculum for gifted and talented students for Baltimore County Public Schools and the Maryland State Department of Education.

COMMON CORE STATE STANDARDS ALIGNMENT

Lesson	Common Core State Standards
Lesson 1.1	RI.5.1 Quote accurately from a text when explaining what the text says explicitly and when drawing inferences from the text.
	RI.5.3 Explain the relationships or interactions between two or more individuals, events, ideas, or concepts in a historical, scientific, or technical text based on specific information in the text.
	SL.5.1 Engage effectively in a range of collaborative discussions (one-on-one, in groups, and teacher-led) with diverse partners on grade 5 topics and texts, building on others' ideas and expressing their own clearly.
Lesson 1.2	W.5.8 Recall relevant information from experiences or gather relevant information from print and digital sources; summarize or paraphrase information in notes and finished work, and provide a list of sources.
Lesson 1.3	RI.6.4 Determine the meaning of words and phrases as they are used in a text, including figurative, connotative, and technical meanings.
	L.6.6 Acquire and use accurately grade-appropriate general academic and domain-specific words and phrases; gather vocabulary knowledge when considering a word or phrase important to comprehension or expression.
Lesson 1.4	W.6.4 Produce clear and coherent writing in which the development, organization, and style are appropriate to task, purpose, and audience.
	W.6.5 With some guidance and support from peers and adults, develop and strengthen writing as needed by planning, revising, editing, rewriting, or trying a new approach. (Editing for conventions should demonstrate command of Language standards 1–3 up to and including grade 6 here.)
	W.6.6 Use technology, including the Internet, to produce and publish writing as well as to interact and collaborate with others; demonstrate sufficient command of keyboarding skills to type a minimum of three pages in a single sitting.

Lesson	Common Core State Standards
Lesson 2.1	L.6.5 Demonstrate understanding of figurative language, word relationships, and nuances in word meanings.
	L.6.5c Distinguish among the connotations (associations) of words with similar denotations (definitions) (e.g., stingy, scrimping, economical, unwasteful, thrifty).
	SL.6.1 Engage effectively in a range of collaborative discussions (one-on-one, in groups, and teacher-led) with diverse partners on grade 6 topics, texts, and issues, building on others' ideas and expressing their own clearly.
Lesson 2.2	RL.6.1 Cite textual evidence to support analysis of what the text says explicitly as well as inferences drawn from the text.
	RL.6.5 Analyze how a particular sentence, chapter, scene, or stanza fits into the overall structure of a text and contributes to the development of the theme, setting, or plot.
	SL.6.1 Engage effectively in a range of collaborative discussions (one-on-one, in groups, and teacher-led) with diverse partners on grade 6 topics, texts, and issues, building on others' ideas and expressing their own clearly.
Lesson 2.3	RL.6.1 Cite textual evidence to support analysis of what the text says explicitly as well as inferences drawn from the text.
	RL.6.3 Describe how a particular story's or drama's plot unfolds in a series of episodes as well as how the characters respond or change as the plot moves toward a resolution.
	RL.6.4 Determine the meaning of words and phrases as they are used in a text, including figurative and connotative meanings; analyze the impact of a specific word choice on meaning and tone.
	RL.6.5 Analyze how a particular sentence, chapter, scene, or stanza fits into the overall structure of a text and contributes to the development of the theme, setting, or plot.
	W.6.4 Produce clear and coherent writing in which the development, organization, and style are appropriate to task, purpose, and audience.
	W.6.7 Conduct short research projects to answer a question, drawing on several sources and refocusing the inquiry when appropriate.
Lesson 2.4	RL.6.1 Cite textual evidence to support analysis of what the text says explicitly as well as inferences drawn from the text.

Lesson	Common Core State Standards
Lesson 2.4, *continued*	SL.6.1a Come to discussions prepared, having read or researched material under study; explicitly draw on that preparation by referring to evidence on the topic, text, or issue to probe and reflect on ideas under discussion.
	SL.6.1b Follow rules for collegial discussions and decision-making, track progress toward specific goals and deadlines, and define individual roles as needed.
	SL.6.1c Pose questions that connect the ideas of several speakers and respond to others' questions and comments with relevant evidence, observations, and ideas.
	SL.6.1d Acknowledge new information expressed by others, and, when warranted, qualify or justify their own views in light of the evidence presented.
Lesson 2.5	RL.6.1 Cite textual evidence to support analysis of what the text says explicitly as well as inferences drawn from the text.
	W.6.2 Write informative/explanatory texts to examine a topic and convey ideas, concepts, and information through the selection, organization, and analysis of relevant content.
	W.6.4 Produce clear and coherent writing in which the development, organization, and style are appropriate to task, purpose, and audience.
Lesson 3.1	W.6.7 Conduct short research projects to answer a question, drawing on several sources and refocusing the inquiry when appropriate.
	SL.6.1 Engage effectively in a range of collaborative discussions (one-on-one, in groups, and teacher-led) with diverse partners on grade 6 topics, texts, and issues, building on others' ideas and expressing their own clearly.
Lesson 3.2	RL.6.1 Cite textual evidence to support analysis of what the text says explicitly as well as inferences drawn from the text.
	RL.6.2 Determine a theme or central idea of a text and how it is conveyed through particular details; provide a summary of the text distinct from personal opinions or judgments.
	RI.6.1 Cite textual evidence to support analysis of what the text says explicitly as well as inferences drawn from the text.
	W.6.7 Conduct short research projects to answer a question, drawing on several sources and refocusing the inquiry when appropriate.

Lesson	Common Core State Standards
Lesson 3.2, *continued*	SL.6.1 Engage effectively in a range of collaborative discussions (one-on-one, in groups, and teacher-led) with diverse partners on grade 6 topics, texts, and issues, building on others' ideas and expressing their own clearly.
Lesson 3.3	RL.6.1 Cite textual evidence to support analysis of what the text says explicitly as well as inferences drawn from the text.
	RL.6.3 Describe how a particular story's or drama's plot unfolds in a series of episodes as well as how the characters respond or change as the plot moves toward a resolution.
	RL.6.5 Analyze how a particular sentence, chapter, scene, or stanza fits into the overall structure of a text and contributes to the development of the theme, setting, or plot.
	W.6.9 Draw evidence from literary or informational texts to support analysis, reflection, and research.
Lesson 3.4	RL.6.1 Cite textual evidence to support analysis of what the text says explicitly as well as inferences drawn from the text.
	RL.6.9 Compare and contrast texts in different forms or genres (e.g., stories and poems; historical novels and fantasy stories) in terms of their approaches to similar themes and topics.
	RI.6.1 Cite textual evidence to support analysis of what the text says explicitly as well as inferences drawn from the text.
	SL.6.1d Acknowledge new information expressed by others, and, when warranted, qualify or justify their own views in light of the evidence presented.
Lesson 3.5	RL.6.1 Cite textual evidence to support analysis of what the text says explicitly as well as inferences drawn from the text.
	RI.6.1 Cite textual evidence to support analysis of what the text says explicitly as well as inferences drawn from the text.
	W.6.2 Write informative/explanatory texts to examine a topic and convey ideas, concepts, and information through the selection, organization, and analysis of relevant content.
	W.6.4 Produce clear and coherent writing in which the development, organization, and style are appropriate to task, purpose, and audience.
Lesson 4.1	W.6.7 Conduct short research projects to answer a question, drawing on several sources and refocusing the inquiry when appropriate.
	SL.6.1 Engage effectively in a range of collaborative discussions (one-on-one, in groups, and teacher-led) with diverse partners on grade 6 topics, texts, and issues, building on others' ideas and expressing their own clearly.

Lesson	Common Core State Standards
Lesson 4.2	RH.6-8.5 Describe how a text presents information (e.g., sequentially, comparatively, causally).
	SL.6.1 Engage effectively in a range of collaborative discussions (one-on-one, in groups, and teacher-led) with diverse partners on grade 6 topics, texts, and issues, building on others' ideas and expressing their own clearly.
Lesson 4.3	RL.6.1 Cite textual evidence to support analysis of what the text says explicitly as well as inferences drawn from the text.
	RL.6.2 Determine a theme or central idea of a text and how it is conveyed through particular details; provide a summary of the text distinct from personal opinions or judgments.
	W.6.3d Use precise words and phrases, relevant descriptive details, and sensory language to convey experiences and events.
	SL.6.1 Engage effectively in a range of collaborative discussions (one-on-one, in groups, and teacher-led) with diverse partners on grade 6 topics, texts, and issues, building on others' ideas and expressing their own clearly.
Lesson 4.4	RH.6-8.1 Cite specific textual evidence to support analysis of primary and secondary sources.
	RI.6.7 Integrate information presented in different media or formats (e.g., visually, quantitatively) as well as in words to develop a coherent understanding of a topic or issue.
	SL.6.1 Engage effectively in a range of collaborative discussions (one-on-one, in groups, and teacher-led) with diverse partners on grade 6 topics, texts, and issues, building on others' ideas and expressing their own clearly.